The Job You Want~ How to Get It

Third Edition

Walter L. Blackledge

Professor of Management
Southern Illinois University

Ethel H. Blackledge

Published by
K26 **SOUTH-WESTERN PUBLISHING CO.**
CINCINNATI WEST CHICAGO, ILL. DALLAS PELHAM MANOR, N.Y. PALO ALTO, CALIF.

by South-Western Publishing Co.
Cincinnati, Ohio

ISBN: 0–538–11260–3

Library of Congress Catalog Card Number: 81–52972

3 4 5 6 7 K 8 7 6 5

Printed in the United States of America

PREFACE

Desirable employment plays such a vital role in life that it should be based on careful preparation, training, and planning. The successful search for a job or self-employment is crucial. The outcome of this search will affect not only our future but also the future of our dependents. Today it is estimated that job changes are expected several times in each worker's life, especially during the developing careers of successful people.

How to find a job, and especially the right one, can be vital. Thus, too, it is vital that we understand the importance that training, education, and career planning have to our future. Today, preparing and searching for a job have increased in importance as most people seek employment at least once in their life. Therefore, advancement in the workplace has assumed a great significance as have job-finding skills and job-holding techniques. It is our belief that this book greatly improves one's abilities and opportunities in this area.

This book is written to assist each job seeker to plan and carry out the quest to find the right job. The authors intend that these pages may speak to persons of any age. To young people, calling attention to what is ahead in the workplace and showing how they may begin early in life to prepare themselves can make the procurement of a job just one part of a planned life career. For those who are experienced, a review of these pages will serve as a reminder of desirable ways to present oneself to a prospective new employer.

The Job You Want — How To Get It can help individuals, both experienced and inexperienced, toward jobs of their choice, and thus toward possibilities for better ways of living. Since work comprises a large part of our lives, obtaining suitable jobs with opportunity for use of interests, abilities, and talents as well as for worthwhile payment and satisfaction is as vital to our economy as it is to each of us who works.

The authors found that businesses share this view and were unanimously helpful in preparing *The Job You Want — How To Get It.* Grateful acknowledgment is made to the following firms that have permitted us to reproduce their employment application forms; they have assisted us toward bringing reality to the vital activity of job seeking: Eastman Kodak Company, General Motors Corporation, and The Prudential Insurance Company of America.

W. L. Blackledge
E. H. Blackledge

CONTENTS

1 You Can Get a Job

Job opportunities are everywhere and for everybody. Today there are over 100,000,000 people in the United States who work. Employers are constantly looking for workers to fill job vacancies. Each day many of these employees quit, retire, transfer, or are promoted. Workers with many different abilities and skills are constantly being hired. Job vacancies occur and must be filled every day. With the help of this book, you can probably fill one of these vacancies yourself.

Yes, there are job opportunities for everybody, and they are everywhere. You need to find the job that will fit you personally; there are a number of jobs that may do this. It is the purpose of this book to help you locate, as well as get, the job that fits you. There are proven ways of finding the type of job you want. You will learn about them in each chapter of this book. If you study the suggestions presented here, you will learn many ways to go about finding and getting the job you want.

Your interests, your education, your training and experience prepare you to take advantage of job opportunities. In addition to your abilities, you need to develop job-finding methods and skills through studying job-finding information. How to look for and get the job you want is very important.

Many jobs are available, but you must know how and where to look for them. There is a good market for employees and a better market for qualified employees. Experience, training, and education will qualify you for greater opportunities. For example, you may want to be an accountant, a store manager, a private secretary, or a management trainee. Each of these jobs, as well as thousands of others, have training positions which prepare you for the occupation or job of your choice. There are thousands of such job opportunities from which you may choose.

Now that you are ready to go into the world of business, government, and industry, you want to find the best job available. Decide what kind of job you want and then work toward getting that job. Such a goal is important. Planning and preparation are needed to achieve any goal, such as the successful building and launching of a space shuttle or the training of an astronaut. To be successful, you must plan and prepare for a job. Achieving your goal requires study, planning, know-how, and practice. This is true whether the goal is cross-country travel, marathon running, a dream vacation, or getting a job.

Decide what you want and then pick your job so that it will lead to the type of position and salary that you want in the future. Finding a job, particularly the right one, is easier and faster if you know what you want and how to get it.

Choose a goal. Once you have done this, prepare your campaign. Present your qualifications to an employer in a way that will show you are willing, qualified, and eager to work.

START AT YOUR EDUCATIONAL PLACEMENT OFFICE

Diana wants a job. She has had one year each of typing, accounting, and data processing. What might be a good way for her to find an entry-level job?

Any schools you have attended, including those giving specialized courses, usually have one or more trained individuals who may lead you toward employment. Such an individual may be a guidance counselor, a coordinator, an instructor, or an administrator. Some schools have placement offices where full-time employees aid students in finding employment.

Counselors, coordinators, instructors, and administrators have many contacts. They are aware of the business firms, industrial organizations, and governmental offices which may need help. They receive employment requests from organizations of all types.

Use your education and experience as well as your interests. Apply these interests to job vacancies if possible. For example, if you like art, you might have a flair for store decorating or arranging window displays. Your instructor, your counselor, and your educational adviser are ready to help you. These individuals should be placed first on your list. Listen carefully to their suggestions and counseling.

Illus. 1-1: Your guidance counselor, instructor, and school administrator are ready to help you begin your search for a job.

Diana wanted to know how to begin looking for an entry-level job in which she could use her skills and abilities. One of the best ways for her to find employment is to get in touch with her adviser, instructor, or counselor. Her training in typing, accounting, and data processing will help to place her in an entry-level job.

In the spaces below, answer the following questions:

A. Name one or more individuals at your school (and their office locations) who can help you with job opportunities.

____

____

B. How may you contact these individuals about your desire for a position?

____

____

GET LEADS FROM FRIENDS, RELATIVES, NEIGHBORS, ACQUAINTANCES

Liza has registered for work at the school placement office. What else might she do to increase her chances of getting a job?

When seeking a job, there are many sources of information a young person may use. Parents and other relatives will probably know much more about the community and what organizations may be hiring than you know. Don't hesitate to let them know what type of work you want.

Many times a large firm will not publicly advertise a vacancy. The personnel officer may choose to fill such a vacancy in another way. Why a company would do so was shown a few years ago when a well-known firm advertised that a certain job was open: over 3,000 people applied for the position, and much unnecessary work and confusion resulted. So it is easy to see how individuals might be of more help than commercial advertising. For example, your friends or neighbors may give you suggestions. Even people with whom you are only slightly acquainted can give information which may be quite helpful. Your club or civic organizations may have job notices posted, or some members may suggest places where your qualifications might be put to use.

Liza, after having registered for work at the school placement office, should use all of the sources that have been mentioned in her effort to find a job.

In the spaces below, complete the following problems:

A. List four friends from whom you might obtain information regarding a place to apply.

1. ____________________ 3. ____________________

2. ____________________ 4. ____________________

B. List two relatives who may help you.

1. ____

2. ____

C. List two neighbors who may make suggestions.

1. ______________________

2. ______________________

D. List two acquaintances who might give you help.

1. ______________________

2. ______________________

E. Tell how your club or civic organization might give you assistance.

____

____

READ THE HELP-WANTED ADS

John is ready to search for a job. What suggestions would you give him regarding the use of local help-wanted advertisements?

In today's world there are thousands of employment opportunities for students who are ready to search for a job, whether they seek part-time work after school or full-time work during summer vacations or after graduation. Your first job will probably be part-time. It should provide you with an income and give you valuable experience.

In part-time positions and sometimes in the early stages of your employment career, income need not be the most important item. For example, a part-time job as a teacher's assistant or assistant in your school office can provide an opportunity to gain valuable experience and training. Such experience and training can prove to be priceless. Thus, if you are entering your first employment, whether it is part-time or full-time, you will need to remember that there are many things that often are of equal importance to the income that is offered.

The best way to utilize the help-wanted advertisements is to read them carefully. Then determine from the job listings which opportunities are best for you, based on your qualifications. Match your education and training with the job requirements listed. At the same time apply realistically any experience you may have to the opportunity. For example, one advertisement read:

> Wanted: High school senior or graduate interested in work as music clerk selling popular records and tapes. Must have strong interest in present-day music.

Maria, who was trained in classical music, felt she could have the job if she applied. However, she did not enjoy popular music, and thus felt that she would not enjoy the work. She mentioned the job to her friend Mark, a fan of popular music. Mark applied for the job and was hired. Later he learned of a classical music vacancy for which Maria applied. She also was hired. Both enjoyed their work because they found it interesting.

All organizations at some time need new employees, and help-wanted advertisements are common ways of contacting job candidates. Information about many part-time jobs, particularly neighborhood jobs, can be found on bulletin boards in such places as grocery stores, recreation facilities, business firms, and post offices.

When you study these advertisements, check them all carefully and apply only for those that are actual business vacancies. Many advertisements ask for a certain sum of money to be paid for training courses; some request that you buy samples of their product. It is always wise to ask the advice of respected individuals before you spend money with the hope of obtaining a position with a business or industry.

John wanted to know if the use of local help-wanted advertisements could help him in looking for a job. It would indeed be a good idea if John studied the help-wanted advertisements in the newspapers. If John wants a full-time or part-time job, he should take the one best suited to his own education, experience, and interests. He may then take the first step toward his lifetime career.

Using the spaces indicated, complete the following problems:

A. Search the help-wanted columns and find an advertisement describing the type of job, either permanent or part-time, for which you might apply. Copy the advertisement below.

____

____

____

____

B. List three sources of help-wanted advertisements available to you where employers describe jobs for either permanent or part-time employment.

1. ______________________________________
2. ______________________________________
3. ______________________________________

VISIT ALL TYPES OF EMPLOYMENT OFFICES

Chuck has always been interested in motors and has almost completely assembled a car from various parts. How can Chuck put such ability to use in obtaining a job?

Government, industry, and business firms are always searching for employees. The opportunities are almost endless. Contact and visit their employment offices. To help you find the right job, a good source of information is the "Yellow Pages" of the telephone book. There you will find a complete listing of concerns handling various types of work or services.

Government agencies–federal, state, county, district, city, township, or village–can be good sources of employment. One method of finding these organizations is the local telephone directory. Nearby metropolitan directories may be found at your local library. In many cases you can obtain a toll-free number which makes it possible for you to contact the agency for a list of current vacancies. Locally you may search for job vacancies by contacting the various agencies, such as the public works department or the recreational department. Post offices generally carry a list of their own job openings. Each government agency generally posts a list of its job vacancies and also lists such vacancies with a central clearing agency.

Getting information about a business concern before you apply for employment is highly desirable because it helps you to match your abilities and interests with those of the organization. The more interest you show in your future employer, the more likelihood you will have of obtaining the position.

You may want to know when a firm was established, where its plants or branches are located, and what it offers in the way of products or services. One source of information is the local library. You may also learn about a particular company or industry either through a personal visit or by writing to the firm's personnel department for information.

It is a good idea to obtain such material and study the organization several days or, if possible, weeks before you apply. In this way, during the interview you may know more about the firm than any other applicant. If you are otherwise well qualified, this knowledge will show that you have a strong interest in the company, and the time previously spent learning about the organization may well tip the scale in your favor so that you will be chosen for the position.

Chuck's problem was how to find a job in which he could use his mechanical ability. If Chuck would search the "Yellow Pages," he could find the names of several businesses or nonprofit organizations that may be in need of someone with his abilities. He may then contact an employment office at any of these listings. If the business or nonprofit organization does not have an employment office, he may submit his application to the individual who is in charge of employment.

In the spaces provided, complete the following problems:

A. List five organizations, businesses, or individuals who may be in need of employees with your abilities.

1. ______________________________
2. ______________________________
3. ______________________________
4. ______________________________
5. ______________________________

B. List two government agencies near you that may be in need of someone with your abilities.

1. ______________________________
2. ______________________________

C. Where may you obtain information regarding the organizations or agencies listed in A and B above?

____

____

____

____

D. Various employers sometimes post job openings at a local post office. Obtain such notices from this or another source and list two jobs for which you might be qualified.

1. ______________________________
2. ______________________________

CONSIDER EVERY POSSIBILITY

Kristen is considering applying for a job at McNeal Construction Company. She knows that the company is too small to have an employment office. What can she do?

When one is in search of a job, it is usual to think of a large firm first. There are, however, many small businesses which offer certain advantages. For example, a small firm may give you more personal attention as an employee. You may be given a variety of work instead of one specialized job, thus letting you use more than one skill. A smaller organization, because it is small, can give you the feeling of "belonging." Your individual ability may be noticed sooner than if you were one of thousands in a larger organization. A small business often does not have as large a number of applicants as a sizable firm; here you may find a job for which no one has applied.

Following are a few types of businesses which you might consider. The businesses may be found in the classified section, or "Yellow Pages," of the telephone book:

Drugstores
Grocery stores
Small department stores
Specialty shops
Gift and stationery shops
Automobile dealers
Banks
Radio or television stations
Insurance offices
Construction companies
Public accounting firms
Hospitals
Real estate offices
Fast-food restaurants

Kristen's problem was how to apply for a job at McNeal Construction Company which was a firm too small to have an employment office. Since Kristen has decided on working for a smaller firm, she may get in touch with the company to find out who does the actual hiring. She may have to apply directly to Mr. McNeal, the owner of the firm.

In the spaces below, complete the following problem:

List three small businesses in your area where your skills might be put to use.

1. ______________________________

2. ______________________________

3. ______________________________

USE AVAILABLE RESOURCES

Tracy plans to register at a public employment agency. She is also considering a private agency. Which would you recommend?

When you are seeking employment, you should without question register at the local state employment agency. State employment agencies are a free service offered to help individuals find employment. Such agencies usually have vast listings of local, statewide, and out-of-state jobs. A counselor or representative at such an office will help you find the position for which you are qualified. One of these agencies is probably located in your area; when seeking employment take advantage of the service it provides and register there.

Private employment agencies are another source of obtaining jobs. A private employment agency is a service business which obtains jobs for individuals for a fee. Some private agencies specialize in certain types of openings such as sales, accounting, or clerical work. In many cases the fee is paid by the employer. In some cases the employer and the applicant share the fee; in others the applicant pays the entire fee. A common fee, for example, could range from 6 to 12 percent of one's annual starting salary. This percentage usually increases in proportion to the amount of income the new employee is expected to receive. If you use the services of a private agency, be sure to find out what the charges are, when they must be paid, and whether they are paid by the employer for some positions. Although the fee may seem high, you pay only if you are placed on the job through the services of the agency.

Tracy wanted to know at what type of employment agency she should register: She could apply to both public and private employment agencies in her effort to find a job. If she wishes a special type of work, it might be to her benefit to look into the advantages of seeking work through a private agency.

In the spaces provided, complete the following problems:

A. List the name, address, and telephone number of a public employment agency which might aid you in your search for work.

____

____

B. List the names of two private employment agencies located in your hometown or in a city near you.

1. ______________________________________

2. ______________________________________

C. If you can find out, state the terms or charges made by one private agency for placement service.

____

____

LET PEOPLE KNOW YOU WANT A JOB

Jeff wants to increase his chances of getting a good job by advertising and wonders how he should go about it. He saw in the local newspaper that each student in the community was to be given free space to advertise for a job. Is this a good method to use?

Advertising in the "Situations Wanted" section of the newspaper is another good job-hunting technique. In some sections of the country, once a year certain newspapers give teenagers an opportunity to advertise for work free of charge. Such a service makes it possible for you to obtain a much wider knowledge of job opportunities, both part-time and full-time.

The type of advertisement you write will most likely depend upon whether you are interested in part-time or full-time employment. A full-time ad might be for an accounting, stenographic, or sales job. Part-time ads may be for such jobs as lawn mowing, babysitting, or basement or garage cleaning.

Another way to advertise your services for full- or part-time jobs is to compose the ads on 5″ by 3″ cards. You might give them as reminders to club members or association officials. Also, you might post them in coin laundries, stores, barber shops, or any place where such advertising is desired or allowed. It is a good idea to update your advertisements frequently to make sure that people know you are still available.

Illus. 1-2: You may post notices in public places to advertise your services for a job.

In any case, keep your advertisements or notices short, clear, and to the point. As soon as you are hired, notify any employment agencies at which you may be registered.

Jeff's problem involved a decision whether or not to advertise for a job; he should indeed use the free space the newspaper has offered to get the job he wants.

In the spaces provided, complete the following problems:

A. Compose a job advertisement you might use if you decided to advertise in a newspaper.

____

____

____

____

B. Prepare a notice or advertisement to be put on a 5″ by 3″ card.

C. List four places in your area where you might post such a card.

1. ________________
2. ________________
3. ________________
4. ________________

YOU COULD BE YOUR OWN BOSS

From part-time office work that she has done, Lori has the idea that she wants to be her own boss. What might she do to accomplish this?

If you like the idea of starting your own business, don't hesitate to investigate the possibilities. Find a need and fill it. The ideas for self-employment are endless. Examples might be baking or candy making at home, repair work, bicycle renting, or a door-to-door service that sells books or cosmetics.

Bruce learned from his part-time job how to sell goods door to door. With the experience he acquired from this job, he began a lawn-mowing service and hired helpers to do the work under his direction, managing the accounting, sales, and financial end of the business himself. He bought used equipment, including a truck, and eventually expanded to a delivery service. A friend of Bruce's had a similar idea and began by renting, and later buying, a used truck to haul trash for residents and businesspeople.

Lori wanted to know how she might start her own business. Lori might start a typing service, typing envelopes, letters, term papers, or manuscripts at home. She might then gradually enlarge her business with photocopiers, duplicating machines, word processors, or any service that might fill the needs of the community. Lori may eventually hire employees as her work needs expand.

In the spaces provided, complete the following problem:

List three different occupations in which you might be self-employed.

1. ____________________

2. ____________________

3. ____________________

MATCH YOURSELF AND THE JOB

Few people know how to get the right job in the best way. But whatever job you want, an opportunity is usually there. Study your past experience, training, and education, and you will find a gold mine of abilities. For example, you may have had job experience in high school office work, in a club, with a school newspaper, as a student tutor, or in charitable or volunteer work.

Amy felt that she was good at selling. When she applied to various companies, however, the same question was asked, "What experience have you had?" Her reply was that she had no experience. She did, however, without realizing it, have experience. Her father had owned a small shop where she had helped customers with problems concerning gift purchases. When Amy was advised to tell of her experience in this area, she was hired at the next place she applied. Here was an example of a young applicant who was quite experienced, but it had never occurred to her to bring her real qualifications forward. So bring out your experience and let your future employer know what you can do for the firm that hires you.

You are now ready to enter the world of business, government, and industry. The job you want is waiting for you. The opportunities are there. Take your education and training, apply the job-getting skills you are learning about in this book to your goal, and the job you want will probably be yours.

PREPARING FOR YOUR JOB

A. List places where you might find posted notices for job openings.

____

____

B. List the names of people in your neighborhood who have been successful in self-employment. Can you determine why they have been so successful?

____

____

____

____

C. Decide whether you would prefer to use a private or a public employment agency. List the reasons for your decision.

____

____

____

2 Have You Set a Goal for Yourself?

WHAT ARE YOU LOOKING FOR IN A JOB?

When Beth applied for a job, the personnel director asked, "What kind of job are you looking for?" What does Beth need to know about herself and her goals to answer such a question?

Choose a goal for yourself. This is important to your future and to your employment opportunities. You should have a series of short-range goals to serve as steps toward a long-range goal that you have chosen. In addition, it is important that your goal be suited to your interests, your skills, your abilities, and your personality.

Once you have established the long-range goal, such as an accountant, business executive, or store manager, the first step is to be sure that this goal is matched with your own interests and abilities. A good way to do this is to take your choice of career and study it to determine the characteristics of the job or profession. These might include being able to meet people, arrange displays, write advertisements, work with figures, or supervise workers.

Make it a part of your career planning to talk to people already working in your chosen profession. The more you learn of the occupation you want to enter, the better it is for you. The climb to your ultimate goal can be broken down into individual parts. Then each part can be a step toward your long-range goal. As a result, each part of your experience and each part of your training and education will help you reach this ultimate goal.

So, first decide on the goal you want to reach – the job at which you will be working five, ten, or fifteen years from now. Write down all the things that interest you so that you can use this information to help you make this important decision. Write down the books you like to read, the hobbies that interest you, the sports you enjoy. Decide if you like indoor or outdoor work. Consider the type of people whose company you enjoy. It is a good idea to list each area in order of preference (1, 2, 3) to determine where your greatest interests lie.

You may find that you are interested in different fields. Many young people find this to be true. If you find your interests and activities vary greatly, think about the occupations you like and list them. Can you answer this question: What type of work does each involve? Whatever your decision, make sure that your ambitions coincide with the organization to which you want to apply. For example, if you dislike writing, it probably would be unwise to apply for a job as reporter at the local newspaper. If you do not enjoy working with people, you would not wish to work with customers in a store.

You will find that when you have a special interest in your work, time will pass rapidly while you are engaged in it, and you will probably be interested in learning more about your occupation. Thus, it is easy to see why the matter of interest is so important in the choice of your goal. Perhaps you are unable at this time to make a decision specifically as to what you want to do. If this is the case, additional education and training will help you work toward a broad goal. Additional work experience can also be helpful. Many times a new interest comes from experience on the job or from additional

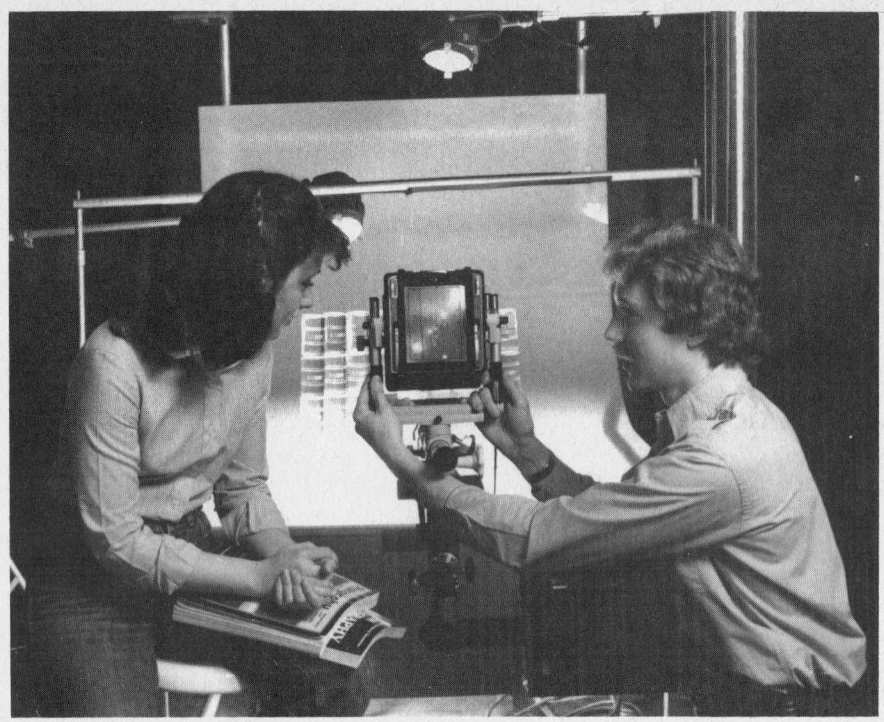

Illus. 2-1: Make it a part of your career planning to talk to people already working in your chosen profession.

education, training, or social experience.

Beth wanted to know how to answer the personnel director's question, "What kind of a job are you looking for?" In answering this question, she should consider her ambitions and interests. Beth has made a list of her interests, skills, and preferences and finds that she enjoys bowling and golf; in school her favorite subjects are in the business field; she prefers working in late afternoon or at night; and she enjoys being with people. Beth has decided that she would like to work in a bowling alley, then manage it, then someday become the owner of a bowling alley. When the personnel director asks Beth what job she would like with the company, Beth may very well answer, "I like business subjects, sports, and working with people. I would like a job in your recreation department." She might also add, "When business is slow, I feel I can save you money by helping with your bookkeeping."

Beth will learn a great deal about people and about recreation in the job she has chosen. Her skills, ambitions, and abilities may eventually lead her toward her long-range goal, whether it is manager of the company's recreation department or the owner of a bowling alley.

In the spaces provided, answer the following questions:

A. List three jobs in order of your preference at which you might hope to be working five years from now.

1. ______________________________
2. ______________________________
3. ______________________________

B. Name three personal qualities or important skills needed for the job or profession which you have chosen.

1. ______________________________
2. ______________________________
3. ______________________________

C. Do you feel that you have or will have these qualities or skills? Explain.

D. List five subjects, activities, or projects in which you are strongly interested.

1. ____
2. ____
3. ____
4. ____
5. ____

E. List three subjects in which you did your best work at school.

1. ____
2. ____
3. ____

F. List three activities in which you have excelled.

1. ____
2. ____
3. ____

G. What do you think are the three best qualities of your personality?

1. ____
2. ____
3. ____

H. What do you think are the three worst qualities of your personality?

1. ____
2. ____
3. ____

I. Explain how you might improve yourself to become better qualified to reach one of the goals you chose in question A.

WHAT CAN YOU DO?

During a job interview Doug was told, "We have a vacancy as a cashier in our cafeteria. We also have a job in the maintenance department which requires work at night and pays a little more." What would you suggest to Doug?

One of the first questions you may be asked in an interview is, "What are you interested in, and what can you do?" If you have not previously anticipated such a question, you may not be able to answer it. It is important that you know your qualifications. These not only include your training but also your job likes and dislikes. Organizations often have more than one vacancy. These vacancies call for different qualifications. The employer is trying to learn either directly or indirectly what your qualifications are, including your likes and dislikes.

It is a good idea to make a list of your abilities, skills, and work preferences. Make a second list of types of work you dislike or for which you feel you are not qualified. In this way you may avoid accepting a job which you dislike or for which you lack qualifications. Your desire to learn at such a job would be handicapped by your dislike and as a result you could not do your best work. Put yourself into work which you enjoy and for which you are qualified and you will do well.

Many young people allow themselves to get into a profession or job to which their personality or aptitude is not suited. Such was the case with Janet. Her father was the owner of a successful clothing store. Janet's father hoped that after his daughter graduated from school she would work for him and eventually take over as manager of his store. Janet was a shy girl who had always been interested in science. Although she had done well in chemistry and physics, she went into selling for the family business to please her father. Customers did not feel at ease with her, nor did she feel at ease with customers. Business began to slow down and everybody was unhappy, particularly Janet. At last her father accepted the fact that she would not become a businesswoman. After obtaining a job as an assistant to a chemist, however, Janet was happy and excelled in her work.

Doug's problem was how to make a choice between two jobs. Doug has listed his likes and dislikes. He found that working with money while having contact with people was a job he enjoyed. Even though the income would be higher from the maintenance job, Doug wanted his evenings free. Also, he believed that his qualifications and interests would advance him more rapidly through the cashier's position. Doug's assumption proved correct. He did a good job when he was hired as cashier. With his ability to deal with people, he was offered a supervisory position in the cafeteria when a vacancy occurred.

In the spaces below, answer the following questions:

A. List five people whom you know who have been successful in their chosen careers and briefly describe each person's job.

1. ______________________________

   ____

2. ______________________________

   ____

3. ______________________________

   ____

4. ____

____

5. ____

____

B. Which of the five types of work that you just listed would you enjoy doing? Why?

____

____

C. Which, if any, would you dislike? Why?

____

____

D. List three subjects in which you did poorly in school or which you did not like.

1. ____
2. ____
3. ____

PREPARE YOURSELF

Before Anne applied for a job, she was told that she would be asked questions which she might consider personal. Why might such questions be asked?

Now that you are on your way toward entering the world of business, you need to know more about yourself. You may at first consider questions asked by an employment manager, a personnel director, or a counselor to be personal, unimportant, or even useless. Let us look into the matter for a moment.

When a job is to be filled, the employer looks for the best possible candidate that can be found for that job. For example, the job may call for someone who is quick with business figures, has the ability to do door-to-door interviewing, or is good working with money. But whatever the job calls for, the employer is seeking to place the right person in that job.

When you are being interviewed by a prospective employer, you may be asked questions which you think are too personal. For example, you may be asked about your medical history or if you have relatives working for the company. The company's policy may require that you be bonded to insure the company against certain types of financial losses such as embezzlement or theft. Thus you might be asked if you are bondable. Some questions may seem more personal to one person than to another. The employer, however, is merely trying to choose the most highly qualified person for the job.

Anne wondered why questions she considered personal might be asked in a job interview. Anne should try to understand and accept the fact that her potential employer is interested primarily in what she can do for the company. Certain questions, many times considered personal by the applicant, are looked upon as routine by the employer.

In the spaces below, answer the following questions:

A. Indicate your class standing (e.g., upper half, upper third).

____

____

B. Has your application for a bond ever been denied?________________

If your answer is yes, explain why.

____

____

____

C. Do you have any medical or physical characteristics that might exclude you from certain types of work?________________

If your answer is yes, explain.

____

____

____

D. Name six of your hobbies and/or extracurricular activities.

1. ________________ 4. ________________
2. ________________ 5. ________________
3. ________________ 6. ________________

E. List four courses you have had that may be pertinent to your application for the job of your choice.

1. ________________________________
2. ________________________________
3. ________________________________
4. ________________________________

F. What kind of work experience (paying or nonpaying) have you had?

G. List three qualifications you have gained through experience.

1. ______
2. ______
3. ______

PREPARING FOR YOUR JOB

A. The personnel director asks if you have any relatives working for the firm. What is your opinion of this question?

B. You find that the job for which you have applied requires that you do hazardous work. Would this change your attitude toward the position? Why?

C. You are told that it will take one year for you to be properly trained for a certain job. You plan to leave the city in approximately that time. What would you tell your prospective employer in such a situation? Explain.

D. The personnel director says, "This job is in a nonsmoking area." Would that be a problem for you? Explain.

____

____

____

E. How would you answer a question concerning your willingness to relocate to another city or to travel 25 percent, 50 percent, or 100 percent of your working time?

____

____

____

____

3 Make Your Summer Profitable

EVERY LITTLE BIT OF EXPERIENCE HELPS

Spring is approaching and Tim and Bonnie are considering summer employment. "Besides the money we'll be making," Tim said, "I wonder what other advantages there might be to working over the summer?"

There are many advantages to summer employment other than that of earning money. Many employers think that work experience is as important as grades or extracurricular activities. For example, one high school student preferred not to work during the summer months. When applying for jobs after graduation, this individual found that employers preferred to hire applicants who had some work experience. Had this person used the summers to gain such experience, it probably would have been easier to find a job after graduation.

There are many other advantages to summer employment. For example, a student who was thinking of going into medicine accepted a job at a hospital. The pay was low, but the special work experience could not be obtained elsewhere. After the summer work experience at the hospital, it became evident to the student that medicine was the field to pursue.

Students often accept a job not only for the work experience and pay but also for vacation conditions that are offered with the position. Summer resorts, motels and camps all over the country are usually in need of qualified people who want jobs for the summer months. For example, a brother and sister accepted work in food service at an exclusive resort. They were given many of the same privileges as the paying guests; they were allowed the use of swimming areas, tennis courts, and golf courses during certain hours. Thus, their summer jobs provided them not only with pay and work experience but also with recreational benefits.

Some students accept jobs in other states or sometimes outside the United States for the summer months. If you are thinking of such a job, you will find that it may present the opportunity for you to travel and also meet people from a different cultural background. At the same time you will be earning money toward your next year of school.

By taking a position in an area of work that you have not previously considered, you may develop a new interest upon which to base your future. For example, Susan was a student who thought she wanted to be a teacher. During one summer, however, she had an opportunity to work in a supermarket where she developed an interest in business management. Susan decided to pursue a totally different type of work through the experience this summer job provided.

Tim and Bonnie wondered what advantages there might be to working during summer vacation. They may consider all the advantages that have been mentioned and then decide what they want – money, experience, vacation, travel, or the chance to meet new people.

In the spaces below, complete the following problems:

A. Describe a type of work which you might be interested in pursuing as a lifetime career.

B. List three temporary jobs for which you might apply which would give you knowledge or experience toward this goal.

1.

2.

3.

C. Tell in what way each job might help you to attain your goal.

1.

2.

3.

D. List three jobs with which you are familiar that might combine vacation, travel, or variety with summer employment.

1.

2.

3.

LEARN WHILE YOU EARN

David has always been interested in social work. He saves all the money he can to further his education in this field. He has been offered two jobs for the summer: a job as an office worker and a job as an assistant in a counseling agency. The work in the office has a higher rate of pay. What would you advise David to do?

If you want to learn about a career in a certain field, get a job in that field. You may accept a job as an office clerk, bellhop, caddy, store clerk, messenger, dining room attendant, or camp counselor. This job may not be the exact position you had decided upon as your ultimate goal; but any job in your chosen field can help you learn more about how to attain the lifetime career position you want.

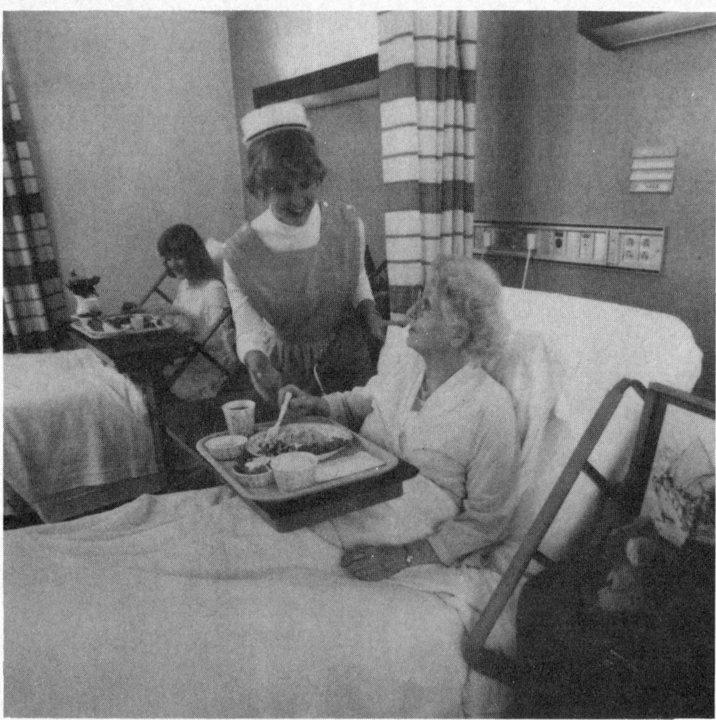

Illus. 3-1: Any job in your chosen field can help you learn more about how to attain the career position you want.

Photo courtesy of Owens-Illinois, Inc.

When seeking a job it is often best to think in terms of your future: At which job can you gain experience toward a lifetime career?

Judy was offered two jobs for the summer. The first was in food service and the second was a job as file clerk at a local insurance company. She felt that the job in food service would pay more than the clerical position. However, she finally chose the second job with the hope of gaining experience and learning more about the business. When the company offered Judy a job for a second summer, she said, "I have learned much about the business through my clerical job, but I would like to learn more through working in another department." Her supervisor asked, "What would you like to do?" Judy answered, "I have learned valuable clerical skills. I'd like to type policies and follow their processing." Because of her interest in the business, Judy was given the job she requested. After her graduation from school, she was given a permanent job with the company and has steadily advanced.

In making your decision about a job, consider not only the pay the job has to offer but also the educational experience it provides. For example, David had to make a decision whether to work for a counseling agency (a job in his field of interest) or take an office job which paid more money. David might find it to his advantage to accept the job at the counseling agency. Here he can get an excellent idea of what work in his chosen field is like while also determining what job possibilities might exist in that field. Although he may not earn as much money as he would in the office job, he may gather information which could be of great value to him at a later time.

In the spaces provided, complete the following problems:

A. List five organizations, firms, or individuals with whom you are familiar who may need employees for the summer months. In each case, tell how your services might be used.

1. ______________________________

____

____

2. ______________________________

____

____

3. ______________________________

____

____

4. ______________________________

____

____

5. ______________________________

____

____

B. Describe a job at which you might earn money and learn at the same time.

____

____

____

BEWARE OF PITFALLS

Jane and Andy found jobs in a local factory during the summer following their junior year in high school. They are attracted by the money they are earning and are trying to decide whether to keep the jobs or return to school in September. What would you advise them to do?

Even though there are many advantages of summer work, there are some disadvantages which you should think about. For example, you might have a most difficult year coming up, feeling that all your subjects are hard. You may feel that circumstances have put you in a position where you have to take too many subjects during the coming year. Or you may feel that since you plan to be quite active in school events, the combination of all the activities will put you under too much pressure. But whatever the reason, it is advisable that you carefully weigh the advantages of summer employment against the disadvantages. If you then decide that summer work is not to your advantage, it is best to postpone it and possibly take a summer course in one of your more difficult subjects.

Don't let money be your only concern in a summer job. You would naturally prefer to work for the highest possible wage during the summer. However, there are disadvantages to a job that is taken or retained only for the wage it has to offer. Such a job is limited in what it can do to help you advance toward your ultimate career goal.

Jane and Andy had to decide whether to keep their summer jobs or return to school in September. It is highly desirable that Jane and Andy return to school. Many students find, after they have accepted a well-paying job before completing their education, that automation or a change in the type of work has replaced them or done away with the job. Then they find that their lack of education keeps them from finding a job elsewhere. If Jane and Andy complete their education, it is very likely that the same company will later accept them for full-time work. With their education completed, they will have an easier time getting a job with another company should the need arise.

In the spaces below, answer the following questions:

A. List five disadvantages you may encounter if you take a summer job.

1. ______________________________

2. ______________________________

3. ______________________________

4. ______________________________

5. ______________________________

B. If you do not work over the summer, what could you accomplish? In what activities could you participate?

____

____

____

____

MAKE YOUR OWN JOB OR CONSIDER AN UNUSUAL JOB

Angela and Mario feel they are not qualified for any particular kind of work. They are, however, good at reading and writing in the Italian language. What would you suggest that Angela and Mario do?

Certain jobs are available because they are so unusual that nobody applies for them. For instance, a student at a southern university accepted the job of feeding and caring for the local mascot, a 350-pound Bengal tiger! One student ran the roller coaster at the local amusement park. Another individual rose every morning at five o'clock to paint oil tanks before the heat of the day. Even in occupations which are very unusual, capable employees are always needed.

Angela and Mario felt they were not qualified for any type of work, even though they could read and write in the Italian language. However, Mario or Angela might serve as a receptionist, member of a hotel staff, a tutor in Italian, or as a clerk in a car rental agency. Mario might read to an older person or a person who is blind whose native language is Italian. Angela might teach Italian to a group of children whose parents may feel that the language should not be forgotten. If they further develop their talent with the language, many interesting jobs requiring knowledge of English and Italian may open for them. This is true for people with bilingual skills in any language. There are many opportunities for those who are bilingual: Airlines, travel agencies, banks, import-export businesses, immigration organizations, and telephone companies all have a need for bilingual employees.

In the spaces below, answer the following questions:

A. List five occupations that could be classified as unique or unusual.

1. __________
2. __________
3. __________
4. __________
5. __________

B. How would you go about looking for one of the unusual jobs you have listed?

____

____

____

C. List three persons with whom you are familiar who have created their own jobs. Explain how those jobs were created.

1. __________
2. __________
3. __________

PREPARING FOR YOUR JOB

A. Think of a trip or vacation you have taken. In what jobs were the persons of your age group employed at the place you visited?

____

____

____

B. Would you consider working at any of these jobs over the summer?

C. In relation to pay, recreation, or experience, what advantages might there be to working at one of these jobs?

D. Describe a summer job that you have had. (This job may have been full-time, part-time, temporary, or perhaps only for a day.) Would you repeat this work or similar work if you had the opportunity? Why?

4 You Can Sell Your Abilities

BEAT THE COMPETITION

Katie applied for an office job. She found the personnel director, due to the seasonal demand, was so overwhelmed with applicants and applications that it seemed an impossible task to handle them. She overheard the director say, "I could use a good typist right now!" What would you suggest that Katie do?

When you apply for work, you should be willing to devote the necessary time to your job. You should be willing to work and learn in an entry-level position. You should be interested in doing the job in the way the boss wants it to be done. You should be willing to work persistently at a task until it is completed. Most importantly, you must convey this quality of willingness to the employer so that you will be remembered. Otherwise, you may be considered just another applicant.

Patrick applied for a position for which he had a strong interest and the needed qualifications. He knew there were other applicants. After the interview, he decided that he wanted the job very much. He believed that he was as well qualified as the other applicants; however, he felt that in his interview he might not have given the employer a strong impression that he was willing to work. When he was notified that two other candidates were being considered, he discussed his feelings with the school counselor. The counselor suggested that he report to the company on the following morning dressed for work. He suggested that Patrick tell the employer that he was qualified and was willing to work the first day without pay to prove he was capable of performing on the job. Patrick agreed to give his time to show that he had the ability to do the job and the willingness to work. With a strong desire to work and a more positive attitude than the other applicants, coupled with equal experience and education, Patrick got the job. Be sure to show a positive attitude. It is in demand.

A good example of how to work toward a specific goal is shown by a story about Theodore Roosevelt. When the President expected a visitor, he would spend long hours reading and studying the subject in which his visitor was interested. In this way he ensured that his talks with visitors would be friendly and productive. A similar approach to learning about a particular employer is helpful to the job applicant. Knowledge about a company can impress an employer because it shows that the job applicant is interested enough in the job to take the time to study and learn about the company and its products or services.

Example after example could be given of the employee who put forth extra effort at work and was rewarded accordingly. The employer's purpose is the production of salable goods or services in a highly competitive market. As a result, each employer needs to find employees who are willing and able to help produce those goods or services at a fair and reasonable price.

Katie had to know a desirable way to approach a

personnel director who was overwhelmed with employment applications. Katie must compete with hundreds of other applicants. If she is to obtain the job, she must show that she is willing to work toward her desired goal. Since the personnel director is obviously in desperate need of help, she might say, "I am ready to go to work *now*. Let me help you with your work." This may give her a small advantage over another applicant. She at least has made an impression that she is ready and willing to go to work. If another candidate is hired, the director may later remember that Katie offered to begin work during a time of need.

In the spaces provided, answer the following questions:

A. List five things you should be willing to do when you apply for a job.

1. ______
2. ______
3. ______
4. ______
5. ______

B. List two ways in which you might show a potential employer that you are willing to work.

1. ______
2. ______

C. How can you make a strong impression upon an employer—as Patrick did—in a way that will get you a job?

______

______

D. Review the technique Theodore Roosevelt used to impress visitors with his knowledge of their field of interest. How might you use this technique in preparing for a job interview?

______

______

______

E. Give two examples of employees who put forth extra effort in their work and explain how they were rewarded.

1. ______

______

2. ______

______

SHOW CONFIDENCE IN YOUR ABILITIES

Lynn applied for a job as sales clerk in a store. During the interview, she kept repeating in a desperate tone, "I *have* to have this job!" What is wrong with Lynn's interviewing technique?

When you apply for a job, the personnel director will want to know about your work experience in order to determine whether you are able to help the firm produce better goods or services. You may be expected to describe whatever skills and abilities you have. You may be asked to explain where and how your training and education were acquired. Employers are always looking for some quality in an applicant that may be of help to the firm.

When you are interviewing with an employer, remember that your attitude may have a lot to do with whether or not you get the job. You should show the employer that you are confident that you can do the job without giving the impression that you are a know-it-all. A friendly and ready smile and a pleasant disposition may also show the employer that you would get along well with the rest of the company's employees. For example, if two people with the same qualifications were being interviewed for the same job, the employer would be more likely to hire the person who showed more confidence and seemed to have a friendly and pleasing personality.

Illus. 4-1: Self-confidence and a positive attitude will help you achieve your personal goal.

Lynn's interviewing technique was to plead with the employer in a desperate tone in an effort to get the job. Lynn is thinking only of herself and her own problems. The personnel director is interested in what Lynn can do for the company, her abilities and skills, and her reliability as an employee. Lynn has to show the personnel director that she is not only willing to work but is qualified for the position. She should emphasize her training in distributive education and her course in retail selling. She should make known to the employer the experience and education she has had that show that she is a qualified applicant. If the employer hires her it will be for her ability to do the job and her reliability. She should emphasize her past work record which indicates that she is punctual and has had perfect attendance on the job.

In the spaces below, complete the following problems:

A. Give two examples of your work experience which show how you might help a company in producing better goods or services.

1. ____________________

____

2. ____________________

____

B. List three different types of training you have had which would be of help to an employer.

1. ____________________

2. ____________________

3. ____________________

C. List two skills you have which you may not have used on a job but which may be of help to an employer.

1. ____________________

2. ____________________

YOU MUST SELL YOUR SKILLS AND ABILITIES

Patricia applied for a job at a television station. The personnel director stated that with her qualifications she would be strongly considered for the position. However, the director was concerned with the problem of employee turnover and wanted to know if Patricia would be a stable employee. Patricia replied, "My husband has two years of college to complete in this town." Did Patricia overcome the personnel director's concern?

Just as a salesperson must show a customer the advantages of buying a particular product, so must you show a prospective employer the advantages of hiring you instead of someone else. You must show the employer that you are willing to work and to learn. Employers desire and need employees who have at heart the interest of the company. By improving your knowledge of the company and helping it to succeed, you are in turn helping yourself to succeed.

Scott wanted a job after school and applied at Mrs. Vartanian's delicatessen. He knew that the delicatessen dealt with a number of people of Armenian ancestry, so before he applied for the job he learned enough words in the Armenian language to greet customers and to express his appreciation for their patronage. When Mrs. Vartanian learned this, she hired Scott in preference to the other job candidates.

Many times selling the importance of a service or product is achieved through merely getting a person to see a problem from a different point of view. For example, Alberto, who owned a small business, had difficulty with Ricardo, an employee. It seemed that Ricardo was an excellent worker but caused arguments between other employees. He pulled practical jokes that subtracted from production time. Alberto, however, believed that Ricardo was an excellent producer and had leadership qualities. He put Ricardo on a pay scale that rewarded him for each piece of work he produced. Ricardo soon eliminated the practical jokes and began to insist that everyone work without argument, since these distractions seriously decreased his pay. Now Ricardo was seeing his job partly from Alberto's standpoint of production and attitude. As a result of the change in viewpoint, production went up and so did profits and morale.

Patricia has already convinced her potential employer of her desirable business qualifications. Her problem is how to answer the employer's questions about the time she will be able to remain on the job. Patricia states, "I will definitely be here for two full years. We are also thinking of making our home here." She has presented her qualifications and indicated a length of service to show the employer the advantages of having her as a worker. When the director realizes that a well-qualified employee is practically guaranteed for at least two years of service, Patricia has an excellent chance of being hired. Her presentation has been a success.

In the spaces provided, answer the following questions:

A. What qualities do you have that can help sell your abilities to a prospective employer?

____

____

____

____

B. Describe three examples from your own experience where a good salesperson showed you what a product or service could do for you.

1. ______________________________

____

2. ______________________________

____

3. ______________________________

____

C. Instead of stating "I worked in a store" in describing your qualifications, how might you restate your experiences and training so that they would sell a future employer on your talents?

____

____

____

D. Improve the following statements of your qualifications.

1. "I am only 17."

____

____

2. "The only place I have ever worked is in my family's dairy business."

____

____

PLAN YOUR ANSWERS

Coretta lives in a large city. She was interviewed for a stenographer's job. Afterward, she said, "The personnel director asked me to list the addresses of all the places I have lived. Why would I be asked to do this?" What would you say to Coretta?

When you apply for a position, your employer will want to know your name, your address, your telephone number, and your social security number. You may also be asked questions which you consider to be more personal: You may be asked questions concerning your hobbies or whether you meet the minimum age standard for the job; for certain types of jobs you may be asked weight and height information.

Most employers will ask for extensive information regarding your education and training. Many of them will ask about your outside activities while you were attending school. Many will ask what you plan to do with your future or what your ambitions are.

No matter how personal you may consider a question, keep in mind that your employer wants to hire the best possible candidate to fill a need in the firm. The interviewer will have a definite purpose in mind, even though to you this individual may seem to be prying for information which you consider too personal to disclose. So be prepared to answer any questions. Know the product you are selling – your own abilities and qualifications for the job!

Coretta wondered why a personnel director would be interested in the places she has lived. There may be many reasons why Coretta's employer wants information regarding her place of residence. If the city in which the firm is located is extremely large, the employment director may want to be sure that she lives close enough to make commuting practical. Also, this employer may have had experiences with former employees not native to the city returning to their hometowns after only a short time with the company. It is certain that the employer has a specific reason for inquiring as to where Coretta has lived and how long she has lived there.

The individuals who do the hiring to fill government jobs may require even more exact information concerning the town in which you have lived, your street address, and other pertinent information regarding your personal history. Such information may be needed for security clearance, to satisfy residency requirements, or to determine your reliability as an employee.

In the spaces below, answer the following questions:

A. What is the status of your health? Excellent ________ Good ________ Fair ________ Poor ________

B. Do you have any physical problems which might keep you from performing certain jobs? If so, explain:

____

____

C. What is your present address?

____

____

D. If hired by this firm, would transportation be a problem for you?

____

____

E. Tell what you do with your spare time, and indicate a specific number of hours per week for each activity which you list.

____

____

____

F. Give two examples with which you are familiar of a prospective employer asking questions which you considered too personal.

1. ____

____

2. ____

____

G. Tell why each firm might have wanted the information which you listed in question F.

1. ____

____

____

2. ____

____

____

DIFFERENT EMPLOYERS ASK DIFFERENT QUESTIONS

Ian applied at three firms for a part-time job. One job involved cleaning windows in a 25-story office building; another required light maintenance work in a bakery; and a third position required maintenance work in a furniture store. Although the jobs for which Ian applied were similar at all three firms, he was asked different questions at each. Why would this be so?

As mentioned previously, an employer may ask many questions which may seem strange to you. You might be asked, "Do you know sign language?" This may seem to have nothing to do with a clerical job or an auto mechanic's job, for example. But it could be very important to an employer who deals with people who cannot hear. A personnel manager might ask if you have ever worked with people who speak a foreign language. Such a question might not seem important to you, but it can be very important to the employer who hires workers to whom English is a second language. A nursery school attendant may ask if you like to work with children. Or a savings and loan company may ask you questions relating to your personal finances and your honesty.

Employers determine what questions to ask by examining the information they need from an applicant to fill a specific job. A good example of why certain questions are asked and how applicants' answers are interpreted was shown recently by an interviewer for an airline. Candidates were being considered for the job of flight attendant. Since the job required extensive travel, the interviewer wanted to make sure not to hire a person who could not bear to be away from home. "Does the idea of leaving your hometown bother you?" one applicant was asked.

"I can't wait until I get out of this town," the applicant blurted.

Thus, the interviewer obtained the information needed as to whether this individual should be hired. "This person may not get homesick," the interviewer explained, "but anyone who is unhappy at home would probably not be happy working for us." So the applicant did not get the job.

Ian was asked different questions when he applied for similar jobs at three different firms. At the places he applied, Ian might be asked different questions for many reasons. The personnel director of the office building might ask him if he has a fear of high places, since he would have to work at different heights in cleaning windows. At the bakery, Ian might be asked if he enjoys the smell of baked goods. At the furniture store, he may be asked questions regarding his physical strength, since he probably will be helping to move large pieces of furniture. So, you can see that each employer needs to obtain different information from Ian even though all three jobs may be quite similar.

In the spaces below, complete the following problems:

A. Name five different types of firms to which you might apply for work.

1. ______________________________
2. ______________________________
3. ______________________________
4. ______________________________
5. ______________________________

B. Give a question that each employer you listed above might ask which would not apply to another type of job.

1. ______________________________
2. ______________________________
3. ______________________________
4. ______________________________
5. ______________________________

"YOU" POWER

Tina has recently graduated from high school. She is now applying for a position as a salesperson at a sporting goods store. What can Tina do for her employer?

It is often said that the most powerful word in the English language is *you*. If you question this statement, take a snapshot of a group of people; then pass the picture around. Who is the first person each individual looks at in the picture? Yes–himself or herself!

Remember this point when you are dealing with a future employer: An employer will be interested when you say, directly or indirectly, "Here is what I can do for *you*." Each employer is working toward keeping the firm efficient and effective in its operation through hiring employees who will effectively help the company.

Many years ago Charles Schwab was paid $1,000,000 a year by Andrew Carnegie. Many people felt that $1,000,000 was too much to pay one person. However, when Carnegie was asked why he paid such a high salary to Schwab, he replied, "Because he is worth twice that amount!" Schwab had qualities to offer that benefited the firm while increasing its profits, and he was paid accordingly.

Remember that owners of firms, managers, and personnel directors are always in search of employees who have qualities which can help the company provide better services or produce better products.

Tina had to convince her employer that she could benefit the firm if she was hired as a salesperson. Tina should tell the employer that she has always been interested in sports. She might also say that she knows many high school students, most of whom may be in the market for sporting goods, and that she feels she could sell to them. If Tina can convince the employer that she can bring customers to the store, she will no doubt get the job.

In the spaces below, answer the following questions:

A. Explain why the word *you* is important.

____

____

____

____

____

B. Do you feel that a person who is paid $1,000,000 a year is overpaid? Explain.

____

____

____

C. List three employers and explain what you could do for each of them.

1. ____________________

____

____

2. ____________________

____

____

3. ____________________

____

____

PREPARING FOR YOUR JOB

A. What is your opinion of an entertainer in Las Vegas receiving a salary of $450,000 per week? Why would an employer pay this amount? What is your opinion of such an employer?

B. Why may XYZ Real Estate Company generally pay its salespeople a commission on each sale rather than a definite salary?

5 Introduce Yourself on Paper

GET TO THE POINT

Debbie is looking for a job and noticed the following advertisement in the local newspaper:

> Mail Clerk. Person to pick up and deliver mail. General clerical duties including filing. Give education. Write: Post-Dispatch, P.O. Box 44.

Debbie is interested in this job and wonders how to begin her letter of application. What would you tell her?

In today's world of employment, much of the searching for employees is done through advertisements. This saves time and expense for the employer and the potential employee. Many times the employer wants to talk only to the candidates with the best qualifications; at these times the employer asks for a reply by mail. Then several potential employees are selected from the application letters and personal data sheets (also called resumes). These are people whom the employer would like to interview. In such cases, the only method of gaining the interview may be through a good letter of application and a good data sheet.

The knowledge and ability to write such a letter, therefore, usually means the difference between getting a number of job offers and not even getting an interview. If the employer is impressed with your letter and data sheet, you could even start at a higher level with more pay than you anticipated.

Since an employer may have several openings and the incoming letters of application may have to be sorted by job classification and sent to the proper person, indicate in your letter which advertisement you are answering and the job for which you are applying. The employer may consider you for a job, or, if you are not hired, your application may be kept for future reference when another opening occurs.

When applying for a job by letter, keep your comments clear and to the point. The person reading your letter may have many other letters to read. Your objective is to get an interview, so present the information in your letter in a manner that will allow it to be read quickly and easily. You may indicate why you think you are qualified for the job, but leave specific data about your education and experience for the data sheet.

Debbie might begin her letter of application for the job she saw in the newspaper as follows: "Please consider me an applicant for the position of mail clerk as advertised in Thursday's *Post-Dispatch*." Debbie has let the firm know specifically that she would like the job of mail clerk; she must now sell the employer on her qualifications and abilities.

In the spaces below, answer the following questions:

A. Find an advertisement that describes a position for which you would like to apply. Put the complete advertisement in the space below by clipping and pasting or by copying the advertisement in the space provided.

____

____

____

____

____

B. How would you begin your letter of application in answer to this advertisement?

____

____

____

____

WHY YOU ARE THE ONE FOR THE JOB

Debbie has begun her letter of application. Now she wants to know what to include in the letter and how to present herself in her writing in a way that will get her an interview. What would you suggest that Debbie do?

Since any letter of application is a sales letter, it is up to you to show your future employer how your education and training can help the firm. Many young people put sales appeal into the first sentences of their application letters while stating the title of the job for which they are applying. For example, a would-be stenographer began a letter of application by writing, "I am applying for the position of stenographer that was advertised in the *Journal* on July 17. I can type rapidly and accurately and take shorthand at a high speed." Another student, who had work experience in the construction industry, began a letter with the question, "Do you have a position for a reliable young person with experience in construction, a steady work history, and excellent references?" Opening sentences such as these cause a prospective employer to give special attention to the letter and data sheet because they imply that the applicants have abilities that would be assets to the firm.

Debbie may want to put sales appeal in her letter. If she decides to do so, she might say, "Are you interested in someone who is a hard worker and who is willing to start at the bottom and learn the business? I majored in business in high school and studied such subjects as filing, accounting, office procedures, and selling. I feel I am the type of employee you are looking for as advertised in Thursday's *Post-Dispatch*."

If Debbie has had any work-related experience, she may want to mention it briefly in the letter to show how it relates to the position for which she is applying. When you write a letter of application, your experience should be listed on your data sheet and mentioned only briefly in the letter. Such experience does not necessarily have to be a regular full-time or part-time job; it might be paying or nonpaying tasks under the supervision of an instructor, counselor, or administrator, or odd jobs you had during the summer.

Sometimes employers may not see how your experience relates to the job vacancy unless it is

Illus. 5-1: You may mention to an employer any work-related experience you have had, even volunteer work at school.

brought to their attention. For example, Debbie might point out that certain tasks she was assigned in a job were difficult but that she was able to complete them successfully. Such a statement in Debbie's letter could indicate that she is both dedicated and resourceful.

In the spaces provided, answer the following questions:

A. In answer to the advertisement you chose at the beginning of the chapter, how would you communicate or sell to your future employer the idea that your training, education, and experience fit the needs of the company?

____

____

____

____

B. Write a sentence or two about your experience that you could use in writing a letter of application for the job you chose at the beginning of the chapter. Mention any work-related experience you have had; explain whether it was in school (such as the school office, with a coach, or for the school newspaper), for relatives, or for a club or other organization with which you were connected.

____

____

____

____

____

C. In another sentence, mention any education or training you have had that might apply to the job in your advertisement. This may have been acquired on the job, in school, through military service, or through a club or other organization.

____

____

____

____

____

TELL THE EMPLOYER WHAT YOU CAN DO

Debbie wants to let her employer know that she is dependable, likes to work, and mixes well with people. How can she do this without appearing boastful?

When you apply for a job, you will probably find that often the little things may tip the scale in your favor. For example, Annette, a high school student, tried to obtain a position in accounting. Because of an illness and several related absences from school, Annette's recent grades had suffered. After being turned down by three firms because of this, she began to feel that the situation was hopeless. While being interviewed at the fourth firm, however, Annette casually mentioned that reading was a personal hobby. When the interviewer asked what kind of books she enjoyed, Annette mentioned books about outstanding people in business, their backgrounds, and about occupations open to professional businesspeople. The interviewer realized that Annette was more interested in the field of business than the grades indicated. She was accepted by the accounting firm and was eventually promoted.

Debbie's problem was how to tell an employer about her personal qualifications for the job without appearing boastful. Debbie should focus on her accomplishments and mention that in high school she helped to deliver the school mail, was elected class treasurer, and was chairperson of the Spring Dance Committee. Such facts in themselves would show Debbie's personal qualifications quite clearly to a prospective employer.

In the spaces provided, answer the following questions:

A. In answer to the advertisement you chose at the beginning of the chapter, list three activities, functions, or groups to which you belong which might show that you like mixing with people.

1. ____
2. ____
3. ____

B. Have you held any kind of office with a student group, club, or other organization? If so, what was the office and what were your duties?

____

____

____

GET PERMISSION FROM REFERENCES

Debbie knows that she should provide her employer with references. She is not sure whether it is acceptable for her references to be relatives or if they should be only business and professional people. She wonders if she should list these references in her letter of application. What would you suggest?

When you apply for a job, you want the employer to develop confidence in your character and abilities. One of the best ways to do this is to provide names, addresses, and telephone numbers of people who know you well, such as a former employer, school official, teacher, or organizational leader. Through contacting these references, the employer can better determine your qualifications for the job.

It is vital that you get permission before giving a person's name as a reference. Make sure the people who have given you permission to use their names know about the job for which you are applying. When the employer contacts them, they can make sure to emphasize the skills and abilities that would qualify you for that particular job.

Debbie need not list her references in her letter of application. Instead, she might mention in her letter that she has received permission to use the references which are listed on her personal data sheet. Debbie can list as references any respected individuals in the community who might be good judges of her character and abilities; however, she should not list relatives.

In the spaces below, answer the following questions:

A. How could an employer gain confidence in you as a prospective employee by talking to a person you gave as a reference?

____

____

____

B. Write a sentence that mentions references on a data sheet that you could include in a letter of application in answer to your job advertisement.

____

____

____

ASK FOR AN INTERVIEW

Debbie wonders how to end her letter of application. What would you suggest?

Your aim in writing a letter of application is to get that all-important interview and the job. To get the job, you must first be in contact with your employer by mail, by telephone, or in person. So, after you have put the necessary information in your letter of application, end the letter by asking that the employer contact you. Make that action as easy for your future employer as possible. Explain how you can be reached and that you are available for an interview.

Debbie could write: "May I have an interview at your convenience? I can be reached by mail at the address at the top of this letter or by telephone at (618) 465-1995."

In the spaces below, complete the following problems:

A. Write a sentence asking the employer in your job advertisement for an interview.

B. Write a sentence telling this employer how you may be reached both by telephone and by mail.

REVIEW WHAT YOU HAVE DONE

Debbie has followed the steps that have been mentioned in preparing her letter of application. Now she wants to put the letter in its final form before sending it to the employer with her data sheet. What is your opinion of Debbie's letter?

When you write a letter of application, make it brief and to the point. It should be typewritten if at all possible; otherwise, be sure that it is neatly handwritten. You need not give full details in your letter. Those may be handled on your data sheet.

It is a good idea to have someone go over your letter to check for clarity, correctness in spelling and grammar, and to comment on the letter's general tone. If possible, choose a person who is capable of writing a good letter and who can read your letter without bias.

Debbie may review what she has written as she completed each step in the making of her letter. She can then put the letter of application in its final form. Her letter will look as shown on page 45.

Complete these two activities:

A. Review the steps you have completed in writing your letter of application. Put the letter together in its complete form in answer to the advertisement you chose at the beginning of the chapter. Attach your final draft of the letter to this page. Use this checklist to make sure your letter is complete:
   1. Mention the specific job for which you are applying and ask that you be considered for the position.
   2. Mention your work experience, education, and training and show how these fit the company's needs.
   3. Describe any activities that show you like mixing with people and being involved in school and community functions.
   4. Mention the references on your data sheet explaining that you have permission to use these names.

5. Ask the potential employer for an interview and tell how you may be reached both by telephone and by mail.

B. Have a friend, relative, or classmate write an opinion of your letter in the space below.

____

____

____

____

____

____

DON'T FORGET YOUR DATA SHEET

Juli wants to apply for the job of secretary. She has written a letter of application and knows that she should enclose a personal data sheet with her letter when she applies for the job. How would you recommend that Juli make up a data sheet?

You should enclose a personal data sheet with your letter of application when you apply for a job through the mail. Such a sheet should be kept to a length of one page. It should include personal information: your name, address, and telephone number. The data sheet should also include information about your education, your work experience, the student activities in which you have taken part, and the special skills you have developed. The names and addresses of people you have asked to serve as references may also be listed on your data sheet.

Juli might make preparing a data sheet easier by breaking the job down into steps.

I. Put the personal information first.

When you apply for a job, you want to make it as easy as possible for your potential employer to get in touch with you; you can do this by putting your name, address, and telephone number at the top of your data sheet. Many applicants find it also to their benefit to volunteer additional information such as age, weight, and height; however, this information is optional.

When Juli completes her personal data sheet (which includes information she has provided on a voluntary basis), the first section should look like this:

PERSONAL DATA SHEET

NAME:	Juli A. Parker		
ADDRESS:	302 North Ninth Street Hamilton, Ohio 45011-9622		
TELEPHONE:	(513) 893-4497		
AGE:	18	WEIGHT:	121 lbs.
HEALTH:	Excellent	HEIGHT:	5 ft. 7 in.

3620 Gary Avenue
Alton, IL 62002-0425
May 15, 19--

P.O. Box 44
c/o St. Louis Post-Dispatch
St. Louis, MO 63118-0457

Ladies and Gentlemen:

Are you interested in someone who is a hard worker and who is willing to start at the bottom and learn the business? I majored in business in high school and studied such subjects as filing, accounting, office procedures, and selling. I feel I am the type of employee you are looking for as advertised in Thursday's Post-Dispatch.

During high school, I helped to deliver the school mail. Last year I was elected class treasurer and was chairperson of the Spring Dance Committee. In each case I enjoyed the work and liked mixing with the people.

On the enclosed data sheet is a list of people who have given me permission to use their names as references.

May I have an interview at your convenience? I can be reached by mail at the address at the top of this letter or by telephone at (618) 465-1995.

Sincerely yours,

Debra A. Johnson

Debra A. Johnson

Enclosure

Illus. 5-2: A letter of application.

In the space below, fill in the blanks to complete the beginning of your own personal data sheet:

PERSONAL DATA SHEET

NAME: ______________________________

ADDRESS: ______________________________

TELEPHONE: ______________________________

AGE: ______________ WEIGHT: ______________

HEALTH: ______________ HEIGHT: ______________

II. Show the subjects you have studied which could help your potential employer.

The employer will probably want to know how much experience Juli has had in shorthand and typing and if she has studied accounting or other business-related subjects.

The next portion of Juli's data sheet would look like this:

```
EDUCATION:  Senior at Hamilton High School, to graduate in June.
            Majoring in business subjects.
SUBJECTS STUDIED:
    Typing:  4 semesters              Consumer Economics:  1 semester
    Shorthand:  4 semesters           Business Math:  1 semester
    Secretarial                       Accounting:  2 semesters
    Procedures:  2 semesters          Business English:  2 semesters
    Business Law:  2 semesters
```

In the spaces below, give information concerning your educational background as shown in Juli's example. List those courses you have studied that show how you might be of help to a potential employer.

EDUCATION: ______________________________

____

____

____

SUBJECTS STUDIED: ______________________________

____

____

____

____

____

____

III. List your student activities.

Let your employer know of any activities in which you have taken part and whether these were in school or outside school. By doing this, you will show that you mix well with people and participate in the activities taking place at school and in your community.

The next part of Juli's personal data sheet would appear as follows:

```
STUDENT ACTIVITIES:  Secretary, Senior Class
                     Vice-President, Future Business Leaders of America
                     Member of Senior Prom Committee
```

In the space below, list in detail any activities (in or out of school) in which you have taken part.

STUDENT ACTIVITIES: ______________________________

____

____

____

IV. Show any special skills you have acquired through training or education.

You may have been trained in business-related subjects or welding, auto mechanics, or other vocational subjects offered in school. Whatever the case, be sure to give your potential employer complete information about your training and abilities.

Juli's data sheet would show the following:

```
SPECIAL SKILLS:  Write shorthand at approximately 110 words per minute.
                 Type at approximately 65 words per minute.  Trained
                 in the operation of adding machine, calculator, and
                 copy machine.
```

In the space below, list any special skills you have acquired through training or education.

SPECIAL SKILLS: ______________________________

____

____

____

____

V. Show any paying or nonpaying work-related experience you have had.

If you have had no full-time work experience, then show what experience you have had, even if it has been acquired through a part-time or nonpaying job. If you have had no work experience at all, then you might list your hobbies instead.

Juli's work experience might appear as follows:

WORK EXPERIENCE:

September 12, 19-- to present: Chemistry Department, Hamilton High School, 1165 Eaton Avenue, Hamilton, Ohio 45013-9624
Duties: Worked as part-time student secretary to Mr. William Elm, chemistry instructor. Took dictation, typed reports, recorded grades.

June 12, 19-- to September 2, 19--: Butler County Park and Recreation Department, 132 Main Street, Hamilton, Ohio 45013-9624
Duties: Full-time general clerical work; operated adding machine, answered telephone, greeted visitors.

In the space below, list your work experience, either paying or nonpaying. Explain what you did on the job and include the dates you worked in each position. If you have had no work experience, list any experience you have had (through hobbies, trips, or school activities, for example) that might show you could be a good employee.

WORK EXPERIENCE: ______________________________

____

____

____

____

____

____

____

VI. Give at least three references.

When you apply for a job, your employer will no doubt want to contact people who know you well to get a better understanding of your character and general suitability for the job. These references may be an instructor, a former employer, or some other respected person in the community.

These are Juli's references:

REFERENCES:

Mrs. Juanita Cox, shorthand and typing instructor, Hamilton High School, 1165 Eaton Avenue, Hamilton, Ohio 45013-9624
Telephone: (513) 869-3240

Mr. William Elm, chemistry instructor, Hamilton High School, 1165 Eaton Avenue, Hamilton, Ohio 45013-9624
Telephone: (513) 869-3240

Ms. Barbara Puccinelli, assistant director, Butler County Park and Recreation Department, 132 Main Street, Hamilton, Ohio 45013-9624
Telephone: (513) 868-1116

In the spaces at the top of page 49, list three references you could use on a personal data sheet. Make sure to give full names, occupational titles, addresses, and telephone numbers.

REFERENCES:

1. ______________________________

____

____

____

2. ______________________________

____

____

____

3. ______________________________

____

____

____

When Juli looks over what she has written in making up her data sheet, she finds that she has a complete list of her qualifications and personal data. She puts this information together to make her data sheet complete. (See Juli's personal data sheet on page 50.)

A. Copy the answers you have written under the headings from I to VI in order to complete your own personal data sheet. Attach your completed data sheet to this page. You will find that you can use this data sheet for any job for which you wish to apply. Have it ready when the next opportunity comes! Take it with you when you apply in person for a job: It will help you in filling out application forms. Below is a checklist of the information you should include in your data sheet as described by the headings I to VI:
   I. Put the personal information first.
   II. Show the subjects you have studied which could help your potential employer.
   III. List your student activities.
   IV. Show any special skills you have acquired through training or education.
   V. Show any paying or nonpaying work-related experience you have had.
   VI. Give at least three references.

B. Have a friend, relative, or classmate look over your data sheet to see if all needed information is present. Ask this person to write some comments regarding your data sheet in the space below.

____

____

____

____

____

____

PERSONAL DATA SHEET

NAME: Juli A. Parker

ADDRESS: 302 North Ninth Street
Hamilton, Ohio 45011-9622

TELEPHONE: (513) 893-4497

AGE: 18 WEIGHT: 121 lbs.

HEALTH: Excellent HEIGHT: 5 ft. 7 in.

EDUCATION: Senior at Hamilton High School, to graduate in June. Majoring in business subjects.

SUBJECTS STUDIED:

Typing: 4 semesters
Shorthand: 4 semesters
Secretarial Procedures: 2 semesters
Business Law: 2 semesters
Consumer Economics: 1 semester
Business Math: 1 semester
Accounting: 2 semesters
Business English: 2 semesters

STUDENT ACTIVITIES: Secretary, Senior Class
Vice-President, Future Business Leaders of America
Member of Senior Prom Committee

SPECIAL SKILLS: Write shorthand at approximately 110 words per minute. Type at approximately 65 words per minute. Trained in the operation of adding machine, calculator, and copy machine.

WORK EXPERIENCE:

September 12, 19-- to present: Chemistry Department, Hamilton High School, 1165 Eaton Avenue, Hamilton, Ohio 45013-9624
Duties: Worked as part-time student secretary to Mr. William Elm, chemistry instructor. Took dictation, typed reports, recorded grades.

June 12, 19-- to September 2, 19--: Butler County Park and Recreation Department, 132 Main Street, Hamilton, Ohio 45013-9624
Duties: Full-time general clerical work; operated adding machine, answered telephone, greeted visitors.

REFERENCES:

Mrs. Juanita Cox, shorthand and typing instructor, Hamilton High School, 1165 Eaton Avenue, Hamilton, Ohio 45013-9624
Telephone: (513) 869-3240

Mr. William Elm, chemistry instructor, Hamilton High School, 1165 Eaton Avenue, Hamilton, Ohio 45013-9624
Telephone: (513) 869-3240

Ms. Barbara Puccinelli, assistant director, Butler County Park and Recreation Department, 132 Main Street, Hamilton, Ohio 45013-9624
Telephone: (513) 868-1116

Illus. 5-3: A personal data sheet.

PREPARING FOR YOUR JOB

A. Denise learned of a job vacancy and wanted to apply. She had some free time in her typing class, so she tore a sheet of paper from her spiral notebook, hurriedly wrote a letter of application, and enclosed the letter in an old envelope she had been carrying in her handbag. No stamp or return address was placed on the envelope. Assuming the letter arrived, what do you think would be the personnel director's reaction to Denise's letter?

B. Discuss the value to yourself and to the personnel director of a well-prepared personal data sheet.

C. Jay read an advertisement for an accounting job which stated, "Please reply in your own handwriting." Jay felt that his writing was poor, so he had a friend write the letter and fill out the application form. Why do you suppose this employer asked for a handwritten reply to the job advertisement? What is likely to happen if Jay is hired? What effect could this have on his standing with the firm?

D. Michael applied for several jobs but neglected to ask his references for permission to use their names. Later he did not call to inform them of what he had done. State your opinion of the recommendations Michael's references will give when they receive telephone calls and letters of inquiry regarding his applications.

6 Your Application Form Expresses You

The job applicant is in much the same position as a salesperson who is selling automobiles, stereos, or any other product. Such a salesperson is competing with other salespeople. So is an applicant competing with other applicants for a job. But instead of selling some product, you must sell yourself—your education, training, and ability to perform some needed service—to a prospective employer.

To be a good salesperson, one must know the best and most appealing qualities of a product. In the same way, you must know your best and most appealing qualities and how to present them so they will gain the favorable attention of an employer.

HOW YOU CAN SELL YOUR ABILITIES

As Gail left to keep an appointment for a job interview, her teacher said, "Now do a good selling job in your interview. Give your application form sales appeal!" Gail puzzled over this. "What am I selling?" she asked herself. "And how do you give sales appeal to an application form?" How would you explain this to Gail?

When selling a product, a salesperson presents that product in the most attractive and most appealing way possible, making it an eye-catching package that will hold the interest and desire of the prospective buyer. So must you, the job applicant, do the same with yourself and your qualifications. By doing this you will be able to compete successfully with others who may be as well qualified or perhaps even better qualified than you are for a certain job. For example, personal sales appeal in an interview is created by a neat and clean appearance, a courteous manner, correct speech, and a pleasant or agreeable personality.

As an applicant you should mention the important facts about yourself and be ready to tell about your experience, your qualifications, and your ability to do the job for which you are applying. You are thereby making yourself a desirable candidate for the job.

Gail wanted to know what she would be selling in an interview and how to give her application form sales appeal. The selling job that Gail has to do in her interview is that of selling her own abilities. If she does it successfully, she will be hired. Gail can give her application form sales appeal by giving careful attention to all the questions asked and by completing all the blanks in the form neatly and accurately.

Complete the following problem:

In the spaces below, list five things you should remember in presenting yourself to a potential employer.

1. ______________________________

____

2. ______________________________

____

3. ______________________________

____

4. ______________________________

____

5. ______________________________

____

THE EMPLOYER WANTS TO KNOW ABOUT YOU AND WHAT YOU CAN DO

After his interview Dan was asked to fill out an application form and send it back to the company. He had given much information to the interviewer already and felt that the application form was not necessary. Do you agree?

Many firms generally require that every applicant fill out an application form. This may be true even if the applicant has applied for a job in person or submitted a letter of application or resume. There are many reasons why companies (especially large ones with hundreds of job applicants) require that application forms be filled out by potential employees.

Many times employers want to make rapid comparisons between applicants and therefore want their own standard application form used. For example, Ms. Ford needed a stenographer who could type especially fast. She examined several application forms completed by persons applying for stenographic jobs. By referring to the same area on each form, she quickly went through dozens of applications, separating all applicants who were only average in typing speed. Thus, there was no need for Ms. Ford to examine data sheets or to read dozens of letters to find out exactly how fast each applicant could type.

The way you fill out an application form can be used to compare you with other applicants. Thus, when you complete the form, neatness, thoroughness, and accuracy are very important. Education and experience can also be readily compared. If two applicants seem to have approximately equal qualifications, but one application form is messy and carelessly filled out, the application form itself might influence the employer in favor of one applicant. One way of being sure that the information you are writing on the application form is accurate is to bring an extra copy of your data sheet with you to an interview so that you have all your information at hand.

Dan wondered why he was expected to fill out an application form after he had already been to an interview. Even though Dan has already given the information to the interviewer, he should fill out his application form carefully, completely, and accurately. He should then send it to the company promptly, making sure that he has attached sufficient postage. By doing this Dan will show much more information about himself than the interviewer could learn just by talking with him. If his application form is complete in all details, it will show thoroughness. If it is well written and neatly typed, it will show his ability to read carefully and complete a task well. If his application form is clean, neat, properly folded, and promptly mailed, it will indicate personal qualities of neatness, promptness, and responsibility. If Dan meets all these requirements, he has an excellent chance of having his application considered favorably.

In the space below, answer the following question:

Why do many employers find it necessary to use standard application forms?

____

____

____

____

THE APPLICATION FORM

In filling out an application form, you are marketing your abilities. Your education, your training, your capabilities, and your willingness to work make up the product you are selling.

But even a fine product can be poorly displayed, carelessly packaged, or look damaged or shopworn and therefore be "undersold." Presenting your assets on the application form indicates to the employer that you are a valuable person to employ. An excellent presentation can make the difference between being hired or put off until another day and turned down completely.

Following are tips to help you give your application blank sales appeal:

I. Always keep the application form neat. If you perspire easily, be sure to keep your hands dry so as not to leave fingerprints or smudge marks on the form. If you fill out the application form at home, use a good typewriter and strive for a perfect copy. If you must make a correction, be sure that it is done

Illus. 6-1: A well-prepared application form is very important; make sure to strive for a perfect copy.

neatly and carefully. Many applicants, when filling out an application form, feel they do their best job by printing. However, you may want to write rather than print the information on the form, if neat handwriting is a requirement for the job. Have a good pen that writes well because this will add to the appearance of your application form.

II. Be accurate. If you are in doubt about something, first write it on a piece of blank paper, then rewrite it on the application form. It is a good idea to read the application through completely and then go back and carefully fill it in. Be sure to have names of people, companies, and locations spelled correctly. If you have doubt about any of the spellings, check them before you apply for the job.

III. Complete the application form by filling in every blank. If you have no answer for some of the blanks (for example, you might be asked about military reserve status when it doesn't apply to you), draw a line through the blank. This will point out that you were thorough and that you did not race through the form and omit something. It also will indicate that you did not, either intentionally or unintentionally, omit answering some of the questions. Many applicants ask for two or three copies of an application form, if they are available. Then the form may be taken home and filled out slowly and carefully so it is complete, accurate, and neatly executed for the employer to consider.

In the spaces provided, answer the following questions:

A. On an application form, what are five ways in which an applicant might attract *unfavorable* attention?

1. ____________________
2. ____________________
3. ____________________
4. ____________________
5. ____________________

B. In what five ways may an applicant give an application form sales appeal?

1. ____________________
2. ____________________
3. ____________________
4. ____________________
5. ____________________

C. Study the application form on pages 57 and 58. Imagine that Gail was given this form to take home and complete. Since no instructions were given that it must be filled out in handwriting, Gail, who will be typing on the job if she is selected, decided to complete the form on a typewriter. (She has also included a resume with her application.) As you examine Gail's completed application, decide what *you* would put into each space about yourself. After you have studied Gail's application form, fill out the blank form that follows it for yourself. Be sure to give your application form sales appeal.

D. In your opinion does Gail's application form have sales appeal? Why or why not?

E. What do you consider to be the best features of the application form you completed?

1.

2.

3.

F. If you were going to fill out another application form, in what ways do you feel that you might improve it?

1.

2.

3.

On pages 62 and 63 is the application form of a large insurance company which Dan has completed. Notice that the statement "Do not write below this line" is present on one of the pages of this form. When filling out an application, make sure to write only in the areas of the form reserved for the use of the applicant. Other areas of the application form will be used by the employer. After you study the application blank which Dan has completed, assume that you are an applicant for a position with the same company; complete the other copy of the form on pages 64 and 65.

On pages 66 and 67 is another application form which you can study. If you have time, fill out the application form for this company. Then have someone inspect your applications to see if they have sales appeal.

UNUSUAL QUESTIONS YOU MAY BE ASKED

Carla's father applied for a job with the purpose of working extra hours in the evening. The application form which he completed asked if he had a license to drive a car. Carla asked her father, "But, Dad, why is it the company's concern whether or not you have a driver's license?"

Many companies need information that might be considered personal by some applicants. These companies need such information for the protection of the firm and other employees. The firm may need to know if an employee will be able to perform certain tasks on the job. If a prospective employee cannot perform such tasks well, that person could endanger other employees or find it impossible to handle the responsibilities of the job.

The company at which Carla's father applied may be looking for an employee to drive executives or visiting businessmen to the airport or deliver products made or manufactured by the firm. Thus it might be imperative for the employee hired for this job to have a driver's license.

Personal Qualification Record

EASTMAN KODAK COMPANY

Date June 15, 19--

Type of Employment Desired: Permanent ☒ Summer ☐ Co-op ☐

1. PERSONAL DATA

Name Shikoku (Last) Gail (First) Elise (Middle) Social Security No. 272-16-8654

Present address, until --- (Date) ; See line below (Street address) --- (City) --- (State) --- (Zip) Telephone No. --- (A.C.)

Permanent address 74 Monroe Ave. (Street address) Rochester, NY (City) 14607-3244 (State, Zip) Telephone No. (716) 315-5154 (A.C.)

Are you able to distinguish colors? Yes Date available to begin employment Immediately

Are you able to remain permanently in U.S.A.? (YES) NO (Circle one) Citizen ☒ PRVisa ☐ Other Visa Status ---

2. EDUCATIONAL RECORD (Basis of Grading System A = 90-100)

School	Name	Years attended From To	Date of Graduation	Degree	Major Subject	Average (% or Point Ratio/Basis)	Class Standing (Upper ½, ¼, 1/10, etc.)
High School	Rochester High School	19-- 19--	6/19--	H.S. Diploma	Business Subjects	85%/B	Upper 1/4
College or University	Ace Business College	19-- 19--	6/19--	Certificate	Business Subjects	90%/A	Upper 1/10
	---	---	---	---	---	--/	---
Post-Doctoral	---	---	---	---	---	--/	---

Thesis for advanced degrees, if any --- Thesis Advisor ---

3. WORK PREFERENCES

Discuss briefly in order of preference, the specific types and phases of work in which you are most interested and believe you are best qualified.

I would very much like to be associated with Eastman Kodak Company. I would like any office position that is available. I wish to make use of my strong interest in business and my previous business training and experience to become a secretary--eventually an executive secretary. Through my business training I have developed skills in shorthand, transcription, word processing, accounting, and office machines. I enjoy working with people and helping them to carry out their duties. I feel that I can make use of my knowledge of the Japanese language in corresponding with various customers or organizations. It is my desire in the future to become an assistant to an executive or group of executives.

Return to:
Personnel Resources
Eastman Kodak Company
343 State Street
Rochester, New York 14650

KP 66877D *An Equal Opportunity Employer — M F* **C**

Illus. 6–2: A well-prepared application (typewritten).

4. SUPPLEMENTARY DATA

Geographic areas in the U.S.A. in which you would **NOT** consider locating None

Have you applied previously for employment anywhere in the Kodak organization? No
If so, state when and where ---

Have you ever worked for any division of the Eastman Kodak Company? No
If so, state where and length of employment ---

Have you worked for any other U. S. firm manufacturing photographic products, synthetic textiles, or plastics? No
If so, indicate firm and length of employment ---

Have you any relatives (first cousins or closer) employed with any U. S. firm of the types just mentioned? No
If so, state where ---

5. SUPPORTING DOCUMENTS

IMPORTANT

The following information must be enclosed to insure complete consideration of your employment application:

1. An up-to-date listing of your college courses and grades (if PhD, only graduate courses and grades are needed).
2. A resume which describes your previous employment, if any, (including military), noting dates, names and addresses, types of positions (indicating full or significant part time employment), salary history and reasons for leaving.
3. A list of campus activities, special achievements, honors and/or publications.

6. PROFESSIONAL REFERENCES

(These references may be contacted unless otherwise indicated.)

Exclude relatives. Give references who are thoroughly familiar with your interests, ability, training and character. These references should be faculty members in your major department and/or employment supervisors who are familiar with your academic or professional work.

1. Name Mr. Lawrence Allen, Ph.D. Street and Number 562 Wilson Street
   Occupation Prof., Ace Business College City, State and Zip Code Rochester, NY 14607-3246
2. Name Mr. Walter Lloyd, Jr. Street and Number 728 Mark Drive
   Occupation Director, Local United Fund City, State and Zip Code Rochester, NY 14650-3242

I hereby authorize Kodak to obtain information from my previous employers and such other sources as Kodak determines to be reasonably necessary in connection with my employment. I understand that falsification of any information submitted to Kodak by me for employment consideration may result in disciplinary action or employment termination if I am subsequently employed by Kodak.

DATE June 15, 19-- SIGNATURE OF APPLICANT Gail E. Shikoku

Illus. 6–2 (continued)

RESUME

GAIL E. SHIKOKU
74 Monroe Avenue
Rochester, New York 14607-3244
(716) 315-5154

CAREER OBJECTIVE:

Trainee with objective of eventually becoming an executive secretary. Desire to utilize training in word processing, shorthand, typing, and data processing.

QUALIFICATIONS:

Have good English skills and knowledge of office procedures, type accurately at 70 words per minute, take shorthand at 110 words per minute, and transcribe accurately. Courses in word and data processing.

EDUCATION:

Ace Business College, 562 Wilson Street, Rochester, New York 14607-3246
Attended August 19-- to June 19--; graduated with A average.
Activities: Treasurer of Commuter's Club.

College Courses:

Filing-A	Word Processing-A	Business English-A
Shorthand-A	Business Math-B	Personnel Management-B
Accounting-A	Office Machines-A	Office Procedures-A
Typing-A	Business Communications-A	Transcription-A

Rochester High School, 126 Eliot Place, Rochester, New York 14607-3244
Attended September 19-- to June 19--; majored in business and secretarial subjects and graduated with B average.
Activities: Secretary of Photographer's Club.

EXPERIENCE:

Ace Business College, 562 Wilson Street, Rochester, New York 14607-3246 September 19-- to June 19--. Duties: Worked as a part-time office assistant. Handled correspondence, typed letters and reports, took shorthand, answered telephone, operated office machines. Salary: Given in the form of a 50 percent tuition reduction. Left this position upon graduation to seek full-time job.

Rochester Local United Fund, 728 Mark Drive, Rochester, New York 14650-3242 June 19-- to September 19--. Duties: Volunteer secretary; handled mail, telephone, solicitations, general secretarial duties. Salary: Nonpaying volunteer work. Left this position to return to school in the fall.

PERSONAL INFORMATION:

Birth Date: July 29, 19-- Health: Excellent
Marital Status: Single Hobbies: Photography, travel, swimming, tennis

References furnished upon request.

Illus. 6–3: A resume (to be enclosed with an application form).

Personal Qualification Record

EASTMAN KODAK COMPANY

Type of Employment Desired: Permanent ☐ Summer ☐ Co-op ☐

Date ....

1. PERSONAL DATA

Name .... (Last) (First) (Middle) Social Security No. ....

Present address, until .... (Date) ; .... (Street address) (City) (State) (Zip) Telephone No. .... (A.C.)

Permanent address .... (Street address) (City) (State) (Zip) Telephone No. .... (A.C.)

Are you able to distinguish colors? .... Date available to begin employment ....

Are you able to remain permanently in U.S.A.? YES NO (Circle one) Citizen ☐ PRVisa ☐ Other Visa Status ....

2. EDUCATIONAL RECORD (Basis of Grading System A = ...)

School	Name	Years attended From To	Date of Graduation	Degree	Major Subject	Average (% or Point Ratio/Basis)	Class Standing (Upper ½, ¼, 1/10, etc.)
High School						/	
College or University						/	
						/	
Post-Doctoral						/	

Thesis for advanced degrees, if any .... Thesis Advisor ....

3. WORK PREFERENCES

Discuss briefly in order of preference, the specific types and phases of work in which you are most interested and believe you are best qualified.

Return to:
Personnel Resources
Eastman Kodak Company
343 State Street
Rochester, New York 14650

KP 66877D *An Equal Opportunity Employer — M F* C

Illus. 6–4: A blank application form.

4. SUPPLEMENTARY DATA

Geographic areas in the U.S.A. in which you would **NOT** consider locating ....

Have you applied previously for employment anywhere in the Kodak organization?..
If so, state when and where ....

Have you ever worked for any division of the Eastman Kodak Company?..
If so, state where and length of employment ....

Have you worked for any other U. S. firm manufacturing photographic products, synthetic textiles, or plastics?................
If so, indicate firm and length of employment..

Have you any relatives (first cousins or closer) employed with any U. S. firm of the types just mentioned? ....
If so, state where..

5. SUPPORTING DOCUMENTS

IMPORTANT

The following information must be enclosed to insure complete consideration of your employment application:

1. An up-to-date listing of your college courses and grades (if PhD, only graduate courses and grades are needed).
2. A resume which describes your previous employment, if any, (including military), noting dates, names and addresses, types of positions (indicating full or significant part time employment), salary history and reasons for leaving.
3. A list of campus activities, special achievements, honors and/or publications.

6. PROFESSIONAL REFERENCES

(These references may be contacted unless otherwise indicated.)

Exclude relatives. Give references who are thoroughly familiar with your interests, ability, training and character. These references should be faculty members in your major department and/or employment supervisors who are familiar with your academic or professional work.

1. Name .... Street and Number ....

Occupation .... City, State and Zip Code ....

2. Name .... Street and Number ....

Occupation .... City, State and Zip Code ....

I hereby authorize Kodak to obtain information from my previous employers and such other sources as Kodak determines to be reasonably necessary in connection with my employment. I understand that falsification of any information submitted to Kodak by me for employment consideration may result in disciplinary action or employment termination if I am subsequently employed by Kodak.

DATE .... SIGNATURE OF APPLICANT ....

Illus. 6–4 (continued)

Prudential The Prudential Insurance Company of America

an equal opportunity employer

Application for Employment

Please print in ink. Please complete the form fully. All information will be treated in strict confidence.

Applicant:

Name — First	Middle	Last	Date of application Mo.	Day	Yr.
Daniel	Nathanial	Bishop	6	17	19--

Current residence address — No.	Street	Apt. no.	City or town	State	Zip Code	Residence since — Month	Year
133	Franklin Ave.	3	St. Louis	Missouri	63101-1122	March	19--

Previous residence/Last five years — No.	Street	Apt. no.	City or town	State	Zip Code	Period of residence/month and year
67	Delmar Ave.	8	St. Louis	Missouri	63100-1124	From Oct. 19-- to Mar. 19--
						From .... 19 ..... to .... 19........
						From .... 19 ..... to .... 19........

Telephone number/include area code	Social Security Number	If hired, can you submit proof of U.S. Citizenship or of lawful alien status which permits you to work in the U.S.?
(314) 741-8230	361-02-7281	☒ Yes ☐ No

Type of work desired/specific skills you wish to utilize	Are you willing to be transferred to another location?
Data Processing Would you consider a different type of work from above? ☒ Yes ☐ No	☒ Yes ☐ No

Previous business experience and service in the U.S. Armed Forces. You may include volunteer experience which relates to the job for which you are applying.

NOTE: Begin with most recent position. Also furnish dates and explanation for each period of unemployment of one month or more.

Name and address of employer/ volunteer organization	Actual dates month and year	Kind of business	Nature of duties	Approx. weekly salary	Cause of leaving
Mack Gift Shop 201 Jackson Drive St. Louis, Missouri 63100-1329	From June 19-- to August 19--	Retail Gifts	Stock Clerk	$105 (part-time)	Returned to school
	From ....19 .... to 19				
	From ....19 .... to 19				
	From ....19 .... to 19				
	From ....19 .... to 19				
	From ....19 .... to 19				
	From ....19 .... to 19				
	From ....19 .... to 19				

Printed in U.S.A.
Comb 654B Ed 2-81 Cat. #719300C **See Reverse side**

Illus. 6–5: A well-prepared application (handwritten).

Education

Names of schools and location/ other than elementary	Course or major subjects	Graduated yes or no	Scholastic standing/ grade average	Degree
O'Fallon Technical School St. Louis, Missouri	Data Processing	yes	Top 25%-B	Diploma
Northwest High School St. Louis, Missouri	Data Processing, Accounting	yes	Top 50%-C+	High School Diploma

Activities — Scholastic, professional, civic, etc./Specify any leadership positions held. **If school activity, indicate high school or college.**/ Organizations or activities which indicate race, religion or national origin should not be identified by name but can be shown by type of organization (e.g., civic, fraternal, social).

School activities, such as elective offices, clubs, athletics, scholastic honors, societies, scholarships, etc.	Professional organizations, community involvement, fraternal and other activities
Baseball (O'Fallon Technical School) Basketball (Captain of team, Northwest High School)	O'Fallon Award for Cooperation and Leadership

Referred for employment by:
☐ High school ☒ Business school ☐ College ☐ Newspaper ☐ Employment agency Name O'Fallon Technical School
☐ Company employee Name — Position — Location —
☐ Other, who? —

Have you any relatives or friends now employed by the Prudential? ☐ Yes ☒ No	If yes, state full name	Relationship	Division
	—	—	—

Have you ever worked for/or previously applied for work at a Prudential office or any of its subsidiaries?	If yes, give date last worked/	Name and location of office last worked/
Worked ☐ Yes ☒ No	—	—
Applied ☐ Yes ☒ No	or date previously applied —	or name and location of office previously applied —

NOTE: Before signing the following statement, please review this application carefully to make certain that you have answered all the questions that apply to you.

I declare that this application presents, to the best of my knowledge, an accurate statement of facts, and I have no objection to the Company's conducting such investigation of these facts as it may deem advisable. This authorization shall be valid for one year from this date.

I understand that misrepresentation or omission of any fact called for hereon, or on any other statements made in connection with my request for employment, will be sufficient cause for dismissal from the Company's service if I shall have been employed.

Applicant's signature Daniel (First) Nathaniel (Middle) Bishop (Last) Date June 17, 19--

Company Use Only/To be completed after employment/Do not write below this line

I have seen .... and am satisfied that .... is employee's correct date of birth: Month Day Year

Interviewer's initials ....

Date appointed Mo. | Day | Year	Reappointment		Code	Salary
	Original appt. date	Department	....	
	Salary consid. date	Division	....	
RHO	Adjusted service date	Section	....	

☐ Reg. ☐ Day ..... Hrs. per day ☐ Temp. ☐ Night ..... Hrs. per wk If change in status check new status ☐ Reg. ☐ FTT ☐ PTT	Title or designation	Title code	Job grp.	Job no.	Job level	Vacancy	Interviewer's initials

Illus. 6–5 (continued)

The Prudential
Insurance Company
of America

an equal opportunity employer

Application for Employment

Please print in ink. Please complete the form fully. All information will be treated in strict confidence.

Applicant:
Name
First | Middle | Last | Date of application: Mo. | Day | Yr.

Current residence address: No. Street Apt. no. City or town State Zip Code	Residence since: Month Year
Previous residence/Last five years: No. Street Apt. no. City or town State Zip Code	Period of residence/month and year From .... 19 ..... to .... 19....... From .... 19 ..... to .... 19....... From .... 19 ..... to .... 19.......

Telephone number/include area code	Social Security Number	If hired, can you submit proof of U.S. Citizenship or of lawful alien status which permits you to work in the U.S.? ☐ Yes ☐ No

Type of work desired/specific skills you wish to utilize Would you consider a different type of work from above? ☐Yes ☐No	Are you willing to be transferred to another location? ☐ Yes ☐ No

Previous business experience and service in the U.S. Armed Forces. You may include volunteer experience which relates to the job for which you are applying.

NOTE: Begin with most recent position. Also furnish dates and explanation for each period of unemployment of one month or more.

Name and address of employer/ volunteer organization	Actual dates month and year	Kind of business	Nature of duties	Approx. weekly salary	Cause of leaving
	From .... 19 .... to 19				
	From .... 19 .... to 19				
	From .... 19 .... to 19				
	From .... 19 .... to 19				
	From .... 19 .... to 19				
	From .... 19 .... to 19				
	From .... 19 .... to 19				
	From .... 19 .... to 19				

Printed in U.S.A.
Comb 654B Ed 2-81

Cat. #719300C

See Reverse side

Illus. 6–6: A blank application form.

Education

Names of schools and location/ other than elementary	Course or major subjects	Graduated yes or no	Scholastic standing/ grade average	Degree

Activities – Scholastic, professional, civic, etc./Specify any leadership positions held. **If school activity, indicate high school or college.**/ Organizations or activities which indicate race, religion or national origin should not be identified by name but can be shown by type of organization (e.g., civic, fraternal, social).

School activities, such as elective offices, clubs, athletics, scholastic honors, societies, scholarships, etc.	Professional organizations, community involvement, fraternal and other activities

Referred for employment by:
☐ High school ☐ Business school ☐ College ☐ Newspaper ☐ Employment agency Name..........
☐ Company employee Name .... Position .... Location ....
☐ Other, who? ....

Have you any relatives or friends now employed by the Prudential? ☐ Yes ☐ No	If yes, state full name	Relationship	Division

Have you ever worked for/or previously applied for work at a Prudential office or any of its subsidiaries? Worked ☐ Yes ☐ No Applied ☐ Yes ☐ No	If yes, give date last worked/ .... or date previously applied	Name and location of office last worked/ .... or name and location of office previously applied ....

NOTE: Before signing the following statement, please review this application carefully to make certain that you have answered all the questions that apply to you.

I declare that this application presents, to the best of my knowledge, an accurate statement of facts, and I have no objection to the Company's conducting such investigation of these facts as it may deem advisable. This authorization shall be valid for one year from this date.

I understand that misrepresentation or omission of any fact called for hereon, or on any other statements made in connection with my request for employment, will be sufficient cause for dismissal from the Company's service if I shall have been employed.

Applicant's signature .... Date..........
First Middle Last

Company Use Only/To be completed after employment/Do not write below this line

I have seen..........and am satisfied that..........
is employee's correct date of birth: Month Day Year

Interviewer's initials..........

Date appointed Mo. / Day / Year	Reappointment		Code	Salary
	Original appt. date	Department	....	
	Salary consid. date	Division	....	
RHO	Adjusted service date	Section	....	

☐ Reg. ☐ Day .... Hrs. per day ☐ Temp. ☐ Night .... Hrs. per wk If change in status check new status ☐ Reg. ☐ FTT ☐ PTT	Title or designation	Title code	Job grp.	Job no.	Job level	Vacancy	Interviewer's initials

Illus. 6–6 (continued)

GM 1416
REV. 6-78
PRINTED U.S.A.

GENERAL MOTORS CORPORATION

APPLICATION FOR EMPLOYMENT

GENERAL MOTORS IS AN EQUAL OPPORTUNITY EMPLOYER

PRINT NAME IN FULL ______ (LAST) (FIRST) (MIDDLE) SOCIAL SECURITY NO. ______

OTHER NAME(S), IF ANY, UNDER WHICH YOU HAVE WORKED OR ATTENDED SCHOOL ______

POSITION DESIRED: FIRST CHOICE ______ YEARS EXPERIENCE ______

SECOND CHOICE ______ YEARS EXPERIENCE ______

EMPLOYMENT DESIRED: PERMANENT ____ TEMPORARY ____ SUMMER ____ DATE AVAILABLE TO START WORK ______ WILLING TO WORK ANY SHIFT? YES ____ NO ____

PERSONAL DATA

PRESENT ADDRESS ______ (STREET ADDRESS) (CITY) (STATE) (ZIP CODE) TELEPHONE NO. ______

PERMANENT ADDRESS ______ (STREET ADDRESS) (CITY) (STATE) (ZIP CODE) TELEPHONE NO. ______ ALTERNATE TELEPHONE NO. ______

ARE YOU A CITIZEN OF THE UNITED STATES? ______ IF YOU ARE NOT A U.S. CITIZEN, DO YOU HAVE THE LEGAL RIGHT TO REMAIN PERMANENTLY IN THE U.S.? ______

HAVE YOU EVER BEEN CONVICTED OF A MISDEMEANOR OR FELONY? YES ____ NO ____ IF SO, COMPLETE THE FOLLOWING: (Do Not Include Minor Traffic Violations)

DATE	OFFENSE	PLACE	DISPOSITION

U.S. MILITARY SERVICE

BRANCH OF SERVICE	FROM	TO	RANK OR RATING	Were you *dishonorably* discharged? Yes ____ No ____

EDUCATION

INSTITUTION	NAME AND LOCATION OF SCHOOL	NO OF YEARS ATTENDED	MAJOR FIELD OF STUDY	DEGREES AWARDED
HIGH SCHOOL				
COLLEGE				
OTHER TRAINING				X X X
				X X X

Illus. 6–7: A blank application form.

EXPERIENCE

HAVE YOU EVER WORKED FOR GENERAL MOTORS? YES_____ NO_____

(PLEASE LIST ALL PREVIOUS EMPLOYMENT AND BEGIN BY LISTING YOUR LAST OR PRESENT EMPLOYMENT FIRST)

EMPL'T DATES FROM	TO	COMPANY NAME AND LOCATION	POSITION	WAGE OR SALARY	STATE DUTIES CLEARLY AND BRIEFLY	REASON FOR LEAVING

IN APPLYING HERE FOR EMPLOYMENT IT IS UNDERSTOOD GENERAL MOTORS RESERVES THE PRIVILEGE OF CONTACTING PAST EMPLOYERS REGARDING REFERENCES. MAY WE ALSO CONTACT YOUR PRESENT EMPLOYER AT THIS TIME? YES ☐ NO ☐

ARE THERE ANY ADDITIONAL COMMENTS YOU WOULD CARE TO MAKE REGARDING YOUR EXPERIENCE OR SPECIAL SKILLS?

WHY ARE YOU INTERESTED IN EMPLOYMENT WITH GENERAL MOTORS?

WHAT DO YOU CONSIDER YOUR GREATEST QUALIFICATIONS?

I HEREBY REPRESENT THAT EACH ANSWER TO A QUESTION HEREIN AND ALL OTHER INFORMATION OTHERWISE FURNISHED IS TRUE AND CORRECT. I FURTHER REPRESENT THAT SUCH ANSWERS AND INFORMATION CONSTITUTE A FULL AND COMPLETE DISCLOSURE OF MY KNOWLEDGE WITH RESPECT TO THE QUESTION OR SUBJECT TO WHICH THE ANSWER OR INFORMATION RELATES. I UNDERSTAND THAT ANY INCORRECT, INCOMPLETE, OR FALSE STATEMENT OR INFORMATION FURNISHED BY ME WILL SUBJECT ME TO DISCHARGE AT ANY TIME. IN THE EVENT THAT I AM EMPLOYED BY GENERAL MOTORS, I AGREE TO COMPLY WITH ALL OF ITS ORDERS, RULES AND REGULATIONS. I HEREBY AUTHORIZE MY FORMER EMPLOYERS TO GIVE ANY INFORMATION REGARDING MY EMPLOYMENT WITH THEM AND IN ADDITION, TO FURNISH ANY OTHER INFORMATION THEY MAY HAVE CONCERNING ME.

APPLICANT'S SIGNATURE____________________ DATE__________

(THIS APPLICATION WILL BE RETAINED FOR ONE YEAR FROM DATE FILED.)

RECORD OF APPLICATION, REFERRALS, DISPOSITION, ETC.

DATE INTERVIEWED________________ INTERVIEWER________________

Illus. 6–7 (continued)

Complete the following problem:

Below are listed many questions that have appeared and still appear on the application forms of various companies. Study these questions to see if you are able to answer them; many or all of these questions may appear on your next application form. If you are not prepared to provide the following information, you may not get the job.

1. Are you a U.S. citizen? ________
   If not, do you have the legal right to remain permanently in the United States? ________
2. Have you ever been convicted of a felony? ________
   If so, complete the following (do not include traffic violations):

   Date: ________________ Offense: ________________

   Place: ________________ Disposition: ________________
3. The company reserves the privilege of contacting past employers to learn of your work history. May we also contact your present employer at this time? Yes ________ No ________
4. Why are you interested in employment with our company?

   ____

   ____
5. What is the salary desired? ________________
6. If you are hired by our company, would you consider employment at another location? Yes ________ No ________
7. If required, would you be willing to work:
   a. Shift work? Yes ________ No ________
   b. Overtime work? Yes ________ No ________
   c. Rotational work schedule? Yes ________ No ________
   d. Work schedule other than Monday through Friday? Yes ________ No ________
   e. Work on holidays? Yes ________ No ________
8. Are you willing to travel? Yes ________ No ________
9. When could you be available to begin work? ________________
10. Do you speak or write a language other than English? Yes ________ No ________
    Name of language: ________________
    Do you speak this language fluently? Yes ________ No ________
11. Do you have a disability which could limit or prohibit your performance of the job for which you are applying? ________
    If yes, describe: ________________

    ____
12. Do you have transportation to and from work? Yes ________ No ________
13. Are you at least 18 years of age? Yes ________ No ________
14. If you are employed at present, why do you wish to change jobs? ________________

    ____
15. Do you have any friends or relatives who work for this company? ________________

    ____
16. Do you have a driver's license? Yes ________ No ________
    Do you own a car? Yes ________ No ________

17. What is your career objective? ____________________

____

18. How much working time have you lost due to illness in the past three years? __________

19. What positions of leadership have you held? ____________________

____

20. Have you had military service? Yes ________ No ________
What branch of service? ____________________
Date of discharge: ____________________

21. If you have not completed high school, circle the last grade of education you have completed: 1, 2, 3, 4, 5, 6, 7, 8, 9, 10, 11, 12.

22. Do you have a high school diploma? ________

23. Indicate degrees taken or other education:
Associate Degree ____________ Major subject: ____________
Bachelor's Degree ____________ Major subject: ____________
Other (e.g. technical or business school): ____________________

Many companies explain on their application forms that if any of the information listed on the form is later found to be incorrect or purposely misleading, you could be dismissed from your job. You could lose your job in this way regardless of the amount of time you have worked for a company or your worth as an employee. Therefore, you should fill out an application form accurately and truthfully. You would not want to be excluded at hiring time because of careless answers or later lose your job after you have received salary increases or promotions.

PREPARING FOR YOUR JOB

A. Kelly has completed an application form. She says, "I feel like I left too many blank spaces. I haven't been to college and I have no work experience. What could I do but leave the spaces blank?" What would you say to Kelly?

____

____

____

____

B. Richard also has filled out an application form. He said, "Why do they ask all the questions about shift work, rotating schedules, overtime, and holidays?" What would you tell Richard?

____

____

____

____

C. Juanita said, "I object to giving permission to allow a potential employer to check my school records, my previous employment record, and my credit history." What would you tell Juanita?

____

____

____

____

7 You Have an Interview – What To Do Now

PREPARE FOR YOUR INTERVIEW

Sheri had an interview at a company which manufactured electronic equipment. She was informed by the placement office that this company was featured in an article in a local Sunday paper concerning items which it manufactures. "Why should I go to the library and read that?" Sheri asked, "I'll only do typing and filing if I am hired. I don't have to know anything about electronic equipment." Do you agree with Sheri?

When you are asked to come for a personal interview, you know that a firm is at least slightly interested in you as a potential employee. During the interview, you have a good chance to increase the firm's interest in you so that they will hire you. Since it may affect your whole future, the interview is an important moment in your life, and it is well worthwhile to make careful, even painstaking, preparation for it.

Try to find out all you can about the firm which has shown interest in you. Learn what products are made or what services are provided by the firm. Find out how long the firm has been in business. Learn if the firm has expanded or varied its operations. Such knowledge will enable you to talk more intelligently with your interviewers, and it will help you to answer this commonly asked question: Why do you want to work for our firm? In addition, in a situation where you are among several applicants who are equally qualified for a job, knowledge about the company will increase your chances of being selected for the position.

Information about various employers may be found in several ways. You may find needed facts at the local library, or you may find it necessary to write or telephone the company itself for literature on the history and organization of the firm. You may talk to various employees who have had a long association with the company. Also, you may find people who have lived in the area for many years who may be able to answer some of your questions. The important thing is that you obtain knowledge and facts so that you can show an interest in your potential employer's business. During the interview you can also say that you have seen the company's products in the marketplace and know how they are used.

Sheri didn't think it would be to her advantage to learn about the company's products before her job interview. However, Sheri would be well advised to take a little extra time to learn something about the company. Her knowledge of the firm and its products would indicate to the interviewer that she is interested enough in the company to make the effort to learn more about it. If her business abilities are equal to those of other applicants, this interest and knowledge might help her get the job over applicants who show less interest in the firm.

In the spaces below, answer the following questions:

A. List five facts which you should learn about a company before you apply or are interviewed for a job.

1. ______________________________
2. ______________________________
3. ______________________________
4. ______________________________
5. ______________________________

B. Assuming you have had at least some advance notice about an interview, where may you obtain the facts mentioned above?

1. ______________________________
2. ______________________________
3. ______________________________

C. Choose a company for which you might want to work and assume that you are scheduled for an interview. You are asked the question, "Why do you want to work for our firm?" Use any of the methods that have been mentioned to obtain up-to-date information about the company, and prepare a written answer to this question.

____

____

____

____

____

____

YOUR APPEARANCE CAN HELP OR HURT YOU

Mary wished to make a good impression during her interview. She went to a hairdresser and had her hair done in a style which she felt was destined to become fashionable. To go with her new hairstyle, Mary bought makeup of a type, texture, and color she had never used. She wore her favorite party dress to the interview, arriving late because of all the time she had spent getting dressed. Will Mary make a good first impression at the interview?

No job applicant can escape making an impression of some sort upon the interviewer. Make sure that the impression you make is a good one! A must is to arrive slightly before the time appointed for your interview. Under *no* circumstances should you be late for the interview! Fairly or unfairly, to the interviewer this will be an indication of your habits. If a real emergency prevents you from arriving on time, let your interviewer know beforehand; however, if you want the job, try not to let this happen.

Illus. 7-1: To avoid being late for your interview, make sure to arrive slightly before the appointed time.

When you go to an interview, wear suitable business clothes. Do not wear clothes that are too casual, such as jeans or an old shirt, and do not wear clothes that are too dressy, such as party or evening clothes. The clothes you wear to an interview do not have to be new, but they should be neat and clean. Neatness and cleanliness cannot be overstressed–this includes teeth, hair, and fingernails, as well as every item of clothing. Remember that first impressions can be crucial.

Any extremes on the part of the applicant, whether in personal appearance or behavior, may cause the interviewer to react negatively. This might cause you not to get the job. Many businesses expect their employees to work with a wide range of people, both within and outside the company. You may be judged on how well you will be received by other people according to what you are wearing and how you behave during the interview. So anything that keeps the interviewer from learning about your qualifications and your ability to do the job should be avoided. An employer is likely to be distracted by such things as conspicuous jewelry, inappropriate clothing, or unusual behavior.

If you are in doubt about any part of your appearance, seek advice from an experienced businessperson. A good motto to remember when you are in doubt as to whether you should wear a certain color or style is *don't*!

During an interview you should not chew gum, eat candy, or display nervous mannerisms such as playing with your hair or tapping your fingers. It is probably a good idea not to smoke, even if the interviewer invites you to do so.

Mary made a mistake in trying new makeup, a new hairstyle, and wearing a party dress on the day of her interview. Mary will undoubtedly make a very poor impression. First, the very fact that she is not on time for the interview will be noticed unfavorably by her potential employer. Mary was overdressed for her interview. She probably looked as though she was going to a party rather than to a job interview in a business firm. Mary should have worn her usual hairstyle and makeup and selected neat, comfortable, business-like apparel to wear to her interview.

In the spaces provided, answer the following questions:

A. What is the first *must* for an interview?

____

____

B. Why is the interviewer's first impression of you so important?

____

____

C. When you apply for a job in business, what should you wear?

____

____

D. What are two qualities that cannot be overstressed in dressing for an interview?

1. ____
2. ____

E. What might you do to learn what is generally worn by the employees of a place where you plan to go for an interview?

____

____

____

F. What should job applicants avoid in their dress?

____

____

G. Name three things that might distract an employer during a job interview.

1. ____
2. ____
3. ____

H. Name five things that you should avoid when being interviewed for a job.

1. ____
2. ____
3. ____
4. ____
5. ____

I. If you are in doubt about what to wear for a job interview or about any aspect of your personal appearance, what should you do?

____

____

WHAT YOU SHOULD KNOW ABOUT YOURSELF

Steven has worked summers but has never held a permanent, full-time job. Because of this, he feels it is unnecessary to note dates and facts about himself and his former work to mention to the employer at his job interview. Do you agree?

Just as you should be prepared to talk intelligently about the firm which might hire you, you should be ready to tell the interviewer or employer all the needed data about yourself. Upon entering the employer's office, you should say something such as, "Good morning! I am–. You asked me to come to see you about an accounting job." Do not sit down until you are invited to do so; then say "Thank you," and be seated. Be ready to answer questions such as these: What are the dates you attended school? What is your work experience? What can you do? Why do you wish to work for us?

In speaking to your interviewer, use good English, speak freely, and avoid using slang expressions. Give facts about yourself without boasting. Do not downgrade your school or previous employers, whether you liked them or not. Just now *you* are being judged, not your school or former employers. If you are asked to take a test or to fill out company forms, do so willingly and readily. Your speech will be an important part of your first impression on the employer, and what you say and how you say it may determine whether the job will be yours. If you cannot keep all the necessary details in mind, this is no disgrace–but you should have them on paper and in your possession at a job interview.

Steven felt it was unnecessary to note facts about himself and his former work for his job interview. However, Steven will risk being embarrassed if he cannot recall or refer to facts about himself. He will hardly appear competent if he should say, "I'll have to ask my mother or dad about that." If he does not know his social security number or some other vital information, it might keep him from getting the job, especially if there is a need to fill the job immediately. A very good idea would be for Steven to fill out a sample application blank, such as one of those in Chapter 6, and have it with him during the interview.

In the spaces provided, answer the following questions:

A. List three persons who would speak well of you and who are competent to judge your character and abilities. (Do not list relatives.)

	Name	Address	Years Known	Business or Position
1.				
2.				
3.				

B. Give information concerning your employment (full- or part-time) during the past five years.

	Employer	Your Position and Duties
1.		
2.		
3.		
4.		
5.		

	Dates Worked Month/Year From-To	Reason for Leaving	Monthly Salary
1.			
2.			
3.			
4.			
5.			

C. What is your social security number? ____________________

MIND YOUR MANNERS

When Jim was called in for an interview, the personnel director said, "You'll find this is the most informal company in the world." Jim, wanting to be accepted, sat back in his chair and slouched, with his feet in a sprawling position. What is your opinion of Jim's actions?

If you appear for an interview and are asked to wait for a period of time, sit or stand with good posture. Do not lean or slouch at any time before or during your interview. Body language can imply a great deal to the interviewer. Your attitude and your manner should be poised and pleasing. A smile is always welcome.

Nervous mannerisms should be avoided, such as fingering your hair, your watch, or your bracelet or ring. Try to be natural and avoid all excess motion. Do not touch objects on another person's desk (such as a pencil or paper) unless you are instructed to do so. Do not place your personal items on a desk unless the desk is reserved for your use. Do not look closely at another person's papers as if reading them; assume that they are confidential.

Illus. 7-2: Your attitude and manner should be poised and pleasing during an interview.

Try to judge when the interviewer wants the interview to end. The interviewer may stand, may extend a hand for a handshake, or may say something such as, "You will be notified within two weeks if you are selected from among the applicants." If the interview is at an end, thank the person in charge and leave without delay.

Do not expect to be hired at the interview, for immediate hiring is seldom done. Most likely, the firm's officials will later review your qualifications along with the impression you made during your personal interview. You will then be notified if the firm wants you as an employee. If you are hired, you may be required to take a medical examination at company expense.

Jim thought that since the personnel director at his interview mentioned that the company was informal, acting very informal was the way to be accepted into the firm. The personnel director may have been correct in saying that the company was the most informal in the world. Jim, however, if he wanted to make a good impression, should have sat upright in his chair, feet together, answering the director's questions carefully and politely.

In the spaces below, answer the following questions:

A. Explain how you should know when to sit or stand during an interview. What should you avoid doing and how should you appear when you sit or stand?

____

____

____

____

B. Why should an applicant avoid reading papers that may be on the interviewer's desk?

____

____

C. Name three things the interviewer may do to indicate to you that the interview is over.

1. ______________________________

2. ______________________________

3. ______________________________

D. What should the applicant do when the interview is over?

____

____

E. What should you expect about being hired directly after the interview?

____

____

F. What kind of examination may be required of you if you are hired?

____

TALKING DOLLARS AND CENTS

Sue was asked by an employer, "What salary would you expect if you were hired for this position?" Sue said, "Whatever you want to pay me." Was this a good answer?

When employers ask about salary, they would like to have at least a general idea as to what the employee would be interested in accepting. Many applicants, upon being asked about salary, become nervous and do not know what to say. Some businesspeople recommend that applicants reply, "I would like to be paid at the going rate for someone with my ability and experience." In this way they are not downgrading their own services, nor are they putting a price on their services that the company cannot pay.

Sue answered, "Whatever you want to pay me," when the interviewer asked what salary she would expect if she was hired by the company. This answer may have made the interviewer believe that Sue placed no value on her own services. It would be more satisfactory for Sue to tell the employer approximately what she would be interested in earning—perhaps on the basis of some increase over her previous earnings. Or Sue might want to say that she expected to be paid at the going rate for someone with her ability and experience.

In the spaces below, answer the following questions:

A. If an employer asked what pay you would expect per month for working at a certain job in which you are interested, what would be your reply? ____________________
What pay would you expect per week? ____________________
Per hour? ____________________

B. On what basis would you explain these rates to an employer?

____

____

____

____

C. Some firms have an *appraisal sheet* or *personal evaluation record* on which the interviewer writes facts about the person being interviewed. On page 78 is an appraisal sheet from a large company. Pretend that an employer is going to complete the sheet after an interview with you in order to rate your personal qualities. Study the appraisal sheet then write some comments below which you hope could be made about you following your interview.

____

____

____

____

____

D. Review the comments you wrote in problem C. Could you measure up to your own completed appraisal? Explain.

____

____

____

EVALUATION

	OUTSTANDING	AVERAGE	POOR	COMMENT
Ability to Talk				
Aggressiveness				
Appearance				
Courtesy				
Enthusiasm				
Intelligence				
Maturity				
Personality				
Poise				

For what type of work is the candidate best suited?

Should we consider further? Yes ☐ No ☐

Remarks:

Interviewed

By __________

At __________

Date __________

Illus. 7–3: An appraisal sheet.

REHEARSE FOR THE INTERVIEW

When Kathy's interview was over, she said to a friend, "Everything was so strange to me. I know I appeared nervous." What might Kathy have done to avoid this feeling?

Practice interviewing for a job with a friend or classmate. Use the appraisal sheet on page 78. At one time be the interviewer; at another time be the applicant. This will be valuable preparation for actual job interviews.

Keep in mind that each interview, including each practice interview, can be a helpful experience. From every interview you will gain knowledge and poise which will help you find the job you want and ultimately reach your career goal.

You may be a highly qualified worker. However, you could fail to obtain a job because of a poor presentation of yourself at an interview–perhaps because of a problem which could easily be corrected if you were conscious of it.

Consider each interview to be a pleasant challenge. There is nothing about an interview that should frighten you, so just relax and stay calm. You'll be able to meet each challenge and complete each interview with improved ability; this will lead you to success and the job you want.

Kathy's problem was how to overcome the nervousness and uncertainty she felt during her interview. Kathy would no doubt have felt and appeared much more at ease had she practiced interviews with a friend, relative, or classmate; by doing this, she would have been ready for the employer's questions and the experience of the interview would have seemed more familiar.

WATCH FOR THESE ERRORS!

Monte had an interview at 9:00 a.m. with Mr. Wyrick, personnel director of DuBois and Company. To arrive on time at his interview, Monte would have had to rise at 5:00 a.m. and pay $4 for bus fare. Instead, he rose later in the morning and rode in his father's car pool. He wore his clothes from the day before, which were wrinkled and somewhat soiled.

Upon arrival at 9:15, he talked readily and easily. When he picked up Mr. Wyrick's pen to complete some forms, he found that the pen wrote poorly. Monte did not know the address of a reference and could not recall the exact date of a previous job. Otherwise the forms were neatly and completely filled out. When Monte decided to smoke, he offered a cigarette to Mr. Wyrick.

Monte liked the company and was interested in the job, but he learned later that another person who was less qualified was hired for the position. Monte said, "The other applicant has friends in the company. I wasn't considered fairly." Do you agree with Monte?

A careful reading of the circumstances of Monte's interview should reveal to you that Monte made at least six rather serious errors. Any one of these errors, although seemingly small in itself, could have influenced Mr. Wyrick to decide that Monte should not be hired.

Complete the following problem:

Review Monte's actions before and during his interview. Monte made six serious errors; see if you can list them below. As you list each of Monte's mistakes, write what he should have done instead to make his interview successful.

1. ______________________________

____

2. ______________________________

____

3. ______________________________

____

4. ______________________________

____

5. ______________________________

____

6. ______________________________

____

AFTER YOUR INTERVIEW

When Julian came home from an interview with a certain firm, he very much wanted a job with that firm. He wanted to thank the employer for the interest and courtesy shown him during the interview. Also, he believed that the firm was interested in his qualifications. However, Julian was also aware that many others had been interviewed for the position. Julian wished to remind the personnel department of his continuing interest, his qualifications, and to say again that he was sincerely interested in the job. Which reminder of Julian's interest would be more effective—a thank-you letter or a telephone call? What would you suggest to Julian?

After an interview, a courteous and valuable job-getting idea is to write a letter to the person who interviewed you. Writing such a letter could accomplish at least three things: It could remind the interviewers of your particular qualifications and continuing interest; it could show them that you can write a well-worded and courteous letter that is complete and neat in every respect (an important job skill); and it can, by repeating your address and telephone number, show once again how easily the firm can reach you and ask you to come to work.

If the letter is typewritten, make sure that it is arranged correctly and free of errors; if it is handwritten, make sure the letter is not only legible but attractive. Spelling, punctuation, and arrangement should be checked at least two or three times.

Julian might write a letter such as the one on page 81. Look at it closely and see if you might use it as a model for a letter of your own.

362 Carol Road
Indianapolis, IN 46206-2922
May 29, 19--

Mr. Edwin Poster
Sterling Company
823 Main Street
Indianapolis, IN 46206-2924

Dear Mr. Poster:

Thank you for interviewing me for a secretarial position with your company.

After discussing this job with you, I am very much interested in your company and in the secretarial job opening. I feel that my secretarial procedures and accounting classes, along with my part-time office work at school, have prepared me for this type of job.

If you need any additional information, I can be reached at the address at the top of this letter or by telephone at (552) 381-7043.

Sincerely,

Julian Romero

Julian Romero

Illus. 7–4: A thank-you letter for an interview.

Complete the following activities:

A. Write a *thank-you* letter that you could use to follow a job interview which you had recently. If you have had no job interview recently, pick a type of work for which you feel you are qualified, and pretend you have been interviewed by an employer who could use your services. Personalize the letter as much as you can. Be sure to express thanks, remind the firm of your qualifications, make it clear that you are willing to work, and show the employer that you are readily available. Attach your final draft of the letter to this page.

B. Have a friend, relative, or classmate write an opinion of your letter in the space below.

____

____

____

____

____

PREPARING FOR YOUR JOB

A. Through the process of collecting information for a purchase, Kim felt she learned much about auto and life insurance. While gathering this material, she also learned of an office job available with an insurance company. Do you think Kim can use the knowledge she acquired to help her obtain the position? How can she do this?

____

____

____

____

B. Joe did some research on how people dress in the business community. He became especially interested in banks and savings and loan companies. At one bank he closely studied the manager, the tellers, and others. He believes he has now learned enough about how banking employees dress to apply at this bank for a job. Do you think his research will prove helpful? What do you think he learned?

____

____

____

C. Linda began to study the help-wanted advertisements. She paid particular attention to salaries paid for different types of jobs. Linda especially studied the weekend newspapers, since they have more advertisements, when making comparisons between the various jobs being advertised. What do help-wanted advertisements tell you about salaries? What about beginning salaries? Do you think Linda learned which professions pay more than others? Do you feel she found out which employees and what types of training or services are more in demand?

____

____

____

____

8 Your First Day on the Job

Your first day at work will be an exciting one. It represents your entrance into an entirely new world. You will probably be told to report to a specific individual, such as the head of the personnel department or the supervisor in the department where you will work. No doubt you will have some sort of orientation period, either with a group of new employees or by yourself. The firm's policies probably will be explained to you.

Your supervisor will help you become familiar with your new surroundings, introduce you to other members of your department, and will demonstrate to you what kind of work you are expected to do and how to do it.

DON'T EXPECT TO LEARN EVERYTHING THE FIRST DAY

Marti came home from her first day on the job. In a discouraged voice she said, "I'll never remember all the things I was told today or the names of all the new people I met!" What advice would you give to Marti?

Your first day on the job may be strange and confusing. If you are a new employee of a large firm, its very size may be awesome to you. You may come in contact with machinery or equipment you have never seen before. You may encounter many situations which are new to you.

But remember that this is your first day on the job, and you are only expected to learn and to work to the best of your ability. Your supervisor knows that the situation is strange to you and will judge you accordingly.

Marti was overwhelmed by all the new things she had to learn and people she had to meet during her first day on the job. Marti should not be discouraged. Her feelings are common to most new employees. No doubt tomorrow Marti will feel that her work is becoming more familiar. Also, she may remember several friendly people and begin to recall their names. Marti will find at the end of two or three weeks that she has become familiar with her surroundings and with her co-workers. She may soon feel like a veteran worker who has settled down to do a job with people who are friends. She should, however, accept the fact that she still has a great deal to learn. She should be ready to accept all instructions and training from her supervisor.

In the spaces below, answer the following questions:

A. Name five situations which you may encounter during your first day on the job which might seem strange or confusing.

1. ______________________________

____

2. ______________________________

3. ______________________________

4. ______________________________

5. ______________________________

B. Give two examples of an experience that was so new to you that you felt overwhelmed by it. This experience may have been on a part-time job, with a social group, in school, or perhaps in a summer camp.

1. ______________________________

2. ______________________________

C. In the situations you listed in problem B, tell how you felt after two or three weeks had passed.

1. ______________________________

2. ______________________________

D. List five words or phrases describing your feelings in either of the situations you listed in problem B. (For example, were you excited, nervous, frightened, or ill at ease?)

1. ______________________________
2. ______________________________
3. ______________________________
4. ______________________________
5. ______________________________

TIME IS MONEY

Nancy has just begun her first job. All employees are given a 15-minute break each morning and each afternoon. Nancy discovers that some people remain out of the office 20 or 25 minutes. What would you suggest to Nancy?

It cannot be overstressed that time is important in business, not only to the firm itself, but to the employee. It is important that you be at work promptly at the scheduled time. If you are allowed a break during your working hours, then you must not take time that does not belong to you from the company by extending that break.

If your quitting time is five o'clock, be prepared

to work until five o'clock. Employees who are not willing to meet the hours demanded of them often find that they have cheated not only the company but also themselves.

Michele was hired as a typist-receptionist in an office where she was the only employee. Her employer was frequently in and out of the office on business and relied on her to manage the office and handle incoming telephone calls. Many times Michele was left alone for hours. She soon began to use the telephone for personal calls when her boss was gone. The office work began to accumulate, and business calls and letters were not answered effectively and promptly. The boss soon discovered that Michele was being paid for time she used to socialize with friends and relatives and that she could not be trusted when left alone in the office. So, Michele, instead of outwitting her boss, found herself out of a job.

Individuals who feel they are gaining by taking excess time from the employer at the beginning or end of a workday or during breaks usually find that they have not gained at all. Many times their behavior shows up on their paychecks, and they wonder why others who have worked steadily got a larger raise than they did.

Avoid following the actions of other employees who take extra breaks, quit early, or loaf on the job. Many times such employees are on the way out of the company. It is a good idea to pick a co-worker with the best work habits and follow that person's actions if you want to do a good job and get higher pay. You may observe the best workers to see how they do their jobs; however, make sure always to follow your supervisor's instructions.

When Nancy began her new job, she found that some employees took breaks for longer periods of time than were allowed. Nancy should take a break only during the 15 minutes permitted by the company. She will find that many employees break company rules, but such inattention to the rules is merely a way of cheating their employer and seldom goes unnoticed or without undesirable results.

In the spaces provided, answer the following questions:

A. Choose a place of employment with which you are familiar, then answer the following questions regarding time:

1. If you were employed at this firm, at what time would you be required to begin work? ________
2. Does this firm give morning or afternoon breaks? ________
   If so, how long is the break? ________
3. What is the quitting time? ________
4. Would you ever work on Saturdays? ________
   If so, how often? ________
5. Would you be required to work on Sunday? ________
   On holidays? ________
6. Would you receive a day or part of a day off during the week? ________

B. List three firms or other organizations where the working hours vary. Explain after each how the hours differ. This could be in days off, vacation time, sick leave, starting time, or quitting time.

1. ________

____

____

2. ________

____

____

3. ____

____

____

C. Considering the working hours alone, for which of the firms in problem B would you prefer to work? ______________________________
Why? ______________________________

DON'T BE AFRAID TO SAY, "I DON'T KNOW"

After her first day on the job, Pearl said, "I'd like to know some things, but I don't want my supervisor to think I'm stupid. So I just listen and let my supervisor talk." What advice would you give to Pearl?

When you begin your new job and are introduced to the workers around you, make an effort to remember their names. This is not easy. But later, when your fellow employees recognize that you remember their names, they will be pleased. This builds good relationships.

Also, don't be ashamed to admit that you don't totally understand the operation of the business. You are not expected to know all the answers.

Paul, on his first job in a factory, wanted to impress his supervisor. So he pretended already to know information about the business which his supervisor wanted to tell him. As a result, he found out later that he had missed vital information he should have learned during his first week. Then, instead of looking like an experienced worker, he appeared to be ignorant.

Don't be afraid that you will be ridiculed if you ask questions. If you don't understand something, let your supervisor know this. Your supervisor will be willing to help you in any way, for it is this person's job to help you learn how to do your work in the best way possible. If you do not ask questions, your supervisor will not know that you do not understand some part of your work.

Many times a company, like a school, prepares literature to inform its employees of procedures, rules, and regulations. If you have obtained a job with such a firm, study its literature to learn what you need to know about the company.

Pearl was afraid that if she asked her supervisor questions it would make her appear stupid. Pearl should ask her supervisor questions about anything she doesn't understand. She should let her supervisor know that she is not familiar with the operation of the company. It is best to admit now that she does not understand something rather than to ask questions later when she is expected to have learned her job.

In the spaces below, answer the following questions:

A. Assume that you are on a new job and you have encountered a part of your work with which you are unfamiliar. To whom would you turn for help?

____

B. Suppose the individual you listed above is out of the area for some time. To whom would you turn to answer your questions?

____

C. Assume you need information regarding something personal at work, such as the nearest place to have lunch. Whom would you ask?

____

D. Give the name of an employer with which you are familiar that prints literature to inform its personnel of company policy.

____

E. In problem D, exactly what information is put into written form for employees?

____

____

____

THERE ARE REASONS BEHIND THE RULES

Melanie, on a new job, feels that some of the rules are unnecessary and even silly. What is wrong with the way Melanie thinks?

On your first job you will probably discover that the rules of the workplace are more strict than those of the schools you have attended. Tardiness or absence by employees can mean loss in terms of production. In certain cases some employees cannot function if other employees are not at work. For example, a switchboard operator who arrives late to work may disrupt or delay company business. The absence of an employee may mean that you must do another person's work as well as your own.

Rules in business are made for a definite purpose and are expected to be obeyed. Safety rules are an excellent example: Such rules are made for your protection as well as the protection of others.

Tony went to the Southwest and obtained a job in the oil industry. He was told that a rule against smoking was strictly enforced. Tony felt that there was no reason why he could not smoke when all his work was out in the open. A few days later, he saw a container of gas, ignited by a spark, explode into the sky. Tony was lucky in this case since he saw why the rule against smoking was rigidly enforced. Other workers were not so lucky. One man had lost his right hand and another had lost an eye because they failed to follow the rules prescribed by the company.

Some firms warn employees if a rule has been broken. Sometimes even a first offense means dismissal. You may be endangering not only yourself but others. Thus, it is best that you learn the rules and follow them.

Melanie felt that some of the rules on her new job were unnecessary and silly. However, Melanie should know that there is a definite reason why the rules are in force. Even when an employee has been with the company a long time, the employee may still not be an adequate judge as to whether a rule is necessary. It is best to comply with the rules even if you are a seasoned employee. After Melanie has been with the company for a while, she will be in a better position to see why the rules are so important.

In the spaces provided, answer the following questions:

A. Name a company rule which might appear to be unnecessary to a new worker. (If you are not familiar with such a company rule, ask a friend, neighbor, or relative for this information.)

____

____

____

B. Why is it necessary that this rule be enforced?

____

____

C. Give an example with which you are familiar where an employee broke a company rule.

D. What penalty was placed on the employee when the rule was broken?

E. Name a rule at a school you have attended which you consider to be vital.

F. Why do you consider this rule to be vital?

EVERYONE STARTS AT THE BOTTOM

Neil has begun his first job. At the end of the first week, he said, "I always have to get drinks for everybody. Why can't I take turns with somebody else?" What would you advise Neil?

Many times the newest employee is chosen as the person to run all the errands. This may mean carrying drinks to the rest of the workers, sharpening pencils, obtaining supplies, answering the telephone during the noon hour, eating earlier or later than the other employees, or running small errands for the boss.

Many employers put new workers through a proving period. Some organizations have special jokes that are used on new employees. For instance, workers at a paper manufacturing company enjoyed playing such a joke in the following way. The company possessed modern machinery and equipment unfamiliar to new employees. A new worker would be sent by co-workers to another department to retrieve a "paper stretcher." The new person would naturally assume a "paper stretcher" to be a piece of equipment that was commonly used at the company, though actually no such equipment existed. The veteran workers at the firm enjoyed the newcomer's being sent from factory to office and back again trying to locate a piece of equipment that didn't exist. You may think such a trick, especially if played on you, is childish. Such jokes, however, should be taken with a sense of humor and enjoyed along with the other employees.

New employees are often tested to see how they will react when assigned certain tasks. How employees get along with others is noted at this time. If new workers cause bickering or refuse to do a job they consider beneath their dignity, they will generally not be given jobs which carry more responsibility and pay.

Throughout your schooling, you probably have known many students who delighted in showing off by refusing to do certain jobs or by arguing with the teacher. Remember that such behavior will not be tolerated in business. When time is wasted, production falls off and danger signals begin to show. As a result, not only is the firm affected but the employees are as well.

Neil didn't like having to run errands for the other employees. However, Neil should accept the fact that he is the newest employee and that he will be expected to perform such menial tasks at least for a time. Neil should show that he is willing to get drinks for his co-workers. In time he will find that another new employee will take over the task, and Neil's attitude will be observed and rewarded.

In the spaces below, answer the following questions:

A. Name six tasks which a new employee might consider to be undesirable or beneath one's dignity though they are part of the employee's learning period.

1. ____________________
2. ____________________
3. ____________________
4. ____________________
5. ____________________
6. ____________________

B. Why should a new employee cooperate willingly in performing such jobs?

____

____

C. When the employee wastes time on the job, what two things are affected?

1. ____________________
2. ____________________

D. Give two examples with which you are familiar where new employees performed jobs which they considered to be undesirable or beneath their dignity.

1. ____________________
2. ____________________

YOUR COMPANY'S SUCCESS IS YOUR SUCCESS

Randall works for a small delivery service and feels that he is underpaid. He says, "When I'm making a delivery, sometimes I stop for a hamburger. Sometimes I even visit my girl friend. Why should I knock myself out on my salary?" What advice would you give Randall?

Business, government, and society need people who do their work effectively and efficiently. Such employees benefit all individuals who are consumers of their products or services and also benefit themselves as employees.

Some years ago a large firm was owned and managed by a demanding person who was avoided by the employees. Trying to outwit their boss, certain employees sent signals to the factory workers when the boss was about to appear. Workers would produce madly until the boss left and then would return to their former inactive state. As a result, the company operated at a loss, and the owner was not sure from day to day if the firm could remain in operation.

Eventually, the owner could no longer afford to stay in business. As a result, the business was closed, putting many people out of work. After weeks of searching for other jobs, many of the employees began to realize that they themselves were in many ways to blame for the failure of the firm. "If we had taken the interest of the company to heart, we would have jobs today," said one employee. "But now it's too late."

So you can see how your company's success is your success. If the company for which you work shows a profit, some of that money may go into your paycheck if you are the person who helped add to that profit.

Usually supervisors know which workers are producing and which ones are not. If they do not know, the company may be operating at a loss or even may be forced out of business. It may take time, but a supervisor usually becomes alert to the poor workers. Such workers are generally the first to be let go when business declines or when more efficient employees are hired.

Also, when poor workers go to their next job, they will be asked for references. Thus, a poor employment history follows a worker, so that employees who are loafers are under a severe handicap in getting any kind of job, to say nothing of a good one.

Randall took personal time during his deliveries because he felt he was underpaid. Randall is probably subtracting from his own salary by wasting the time of the company. If he makes fewer deliveries because he stops for a hamburger or visits his girl friend, then the company is receiving less money for the services it offers. As a result, Randall's boss probably feels that he cannot afford to pay Randall a higher wage or consider him for a promotion. It is quite likely that Randall will be one of the first to be laid off if business declines; thus Randall has endangered not only his present but his future chance of obtaining a better job. If Randall worked harder toward giving the service for which he is paid, it is likely that his pay would be increased when the profits of the firm are increased.

In the spaces provided, answer the following questions:

A. In an example above it was shown how certain factory workers tried to outwit their boss. How did they try to do this?

____

____

B. What was the result?

____

____

C. How were the employees themselves to blame?

____

____

D. If employees loaf on the job, what actually are they risking?

____

____

THE HARDER YOU WORK, THE FARTHER YOU GO

During her first day on the job, Gwen saw an announcement that the company offered after-hours training classes so that employees might learn more about the work of their departments and the business as a whole. Gwen hoped that she would not be asked to join a class since she enjoyed being at home evenings and would not want to miss her favorite television programs. She felt that she didn't need such classes because someday she planned to study at a university for a degree. What would you suggest to Gwen?

During your first day on a new job, you will not wish to sign up for classes. You will doubtless want to become familiar with your job and then see what your needs may be. After thinking things over, you can decide what may be the best way to improve yourself. But self-improvement surely should be part of your plans.

In improving yourself and learning more, you will become of more value to the company and will be ready to move ahead when your chance comes. And, of course, more chances come to those who are better prepared than the average worker. You will discover the truth of these sayings: I notice that the harder I work, the luckier I get! *and* The future belongs to those who prepare for it.

Gwen was reluctant to take company training classes after hours. Gwen should realize that whether personal improvement is to be accomplished in company classes or at a university, the decision will be hers to make—as it will be yours when you make plans for your future. Just one word of caution: Don't let the reality of an immediate opportunity go by for the lazy comfort of every evening at home or for great dreams of a wonderful education sometime in the future.

Illus. 8-1: The reward for all your efforts: a first paycheck.

In the spaces below, answer the following questions:

A. On your first day at work, why might you not want to sign up for an after-hours training class?

____

____

B. At what job would you like to be working five years from today?

____

____

C. What would you like to be doing fifteen years from today?

____

____

D. How do you intend to become prepared for the best position in your chosen field?

Remember that the impression you make on other people at work is very important. Arrive at work on time, develop a good work attitude, and do not waste time while on the job. Your supervisors are aware of how well you are doing your work. Their job is to observe employees in order to help them do their jobs more efficiently. Show your supervisor that you can handle the responsibility given to you and that you are interested in self-improvement. You will be recognized for your good work with extra raises and promotions.

You should also keep a positive work attitude, making yourself a pleasant person with whom to work. Many times how well you get along with other people can affect whether or not you get an important promotion.

So now that you have studied this book, you should have some good ideas of how to get a job that you will like. Good wishes for a wonderful, successful career!

PREPARING FOR YOUR JOB

A. Louis was given two booklets, one on company policy and another on company safety rules. He signed a statement saying that he had read both booklets. One safety rule for the area in which he worked was not to wear loose clothing or finger rings. Louis soon discovered that he should have studied the safety manual as well as the company policy book. His ring became caught in a piece of equipment and he nearly lost a finger. Discuss the value of studying company policy and safety rules.

B. Tom has found that on his new job he must make coffee for the other employees. Tom says he does not drink coffee and feels that much of his training is being wasted with menial tasks. He has begun to spend more time in the lounge than his morning break allows, and on his way to make coffee he detours through the accounting department to stop and talk with friends. What is your opinion of Tom's actions?

C. Teri has been hired by a company which pays the tuition for employees who want to continue education at the college level. Teri wants to accept this offer for college since it will help her to advance, but she feels that study combined with work may be too heavy a load for her. What is your opinion of what Teri should do?